Getting Started in Radio

Studymates

25 Key Topics in Business Studies
25 Key Topics in Human Resources
25 Key Topics in Marketing
Accident & Emergency Nursing
Business Organisation
Cultural Studies
English Legal System
European Reformation
Genetics
Macroeconomics
Organic Chemistry
Practical Drama & Theatre Arts
Revolutionary Conflicts
Social Anthropology
Social Statistics
Speaking Better French
Speaking English
Studying Chaucer
Studying History
Studying Literature
Studying Poetry
Understanding Maths
Using Information Technology

Many other titles in preparation

Studymates

Getting Started in Radio

John Florance

www.studymates.co.uk

For Ann with love

First published in 2002 by Studymates Limited, PO Box 2, Taunton, Somerset TA3 3YE, United Kingdom

Telephone: (01823) 432002
Fax: (01823) 430097

Additional educational author, Graham Lawlor

Typeset by PDQ Typesetting, Newcastle-under-Lyme
Printed and bound by Bell & Bain Ltd, Glasgow

Contents

Acknowledgements 8

Introduction **9**
What a presenter needs 10

1 Starting out **15**
The ways in 15
Listening and learning 16
Active listening 17
Gaining experience 20
Case studies 23

2 How to conduct an interview **28**
There are no golden rules 28
What kind of interview? 29
The importance of preparation 31
Cues 32
Researching an interview 36
Putting the interviewee at ease 37
Down the line/phone interviews 40
Questions 41
'Bread and butter' interviews 44
Talking books 44

3 Politicians, pressure groups and powerful people **49**
Who needs 'hard' questioning? 49
What is a 'hard' interview? 50
Preparation 51
Questions 55
Tone 57
Breaking the rules 61
Pressure groups 63
Impartiality 64

4	**The phone-in**	**67**
	The importance of the phone-in	67
	The production of phone-ins	69
	Kinds of phone-in	70
	Case study	75
	Final thoughts	78
5	**Broadcasting and the law**	**81**
	Knowledge of the law	81
	Defamation	82
	Other matters relating to defamation	86
	The law of contempt	88
	Case study	88
	Conclusion	90
6	**Expect the unexpected**	**92**
	Control	92
	Everyday pressure	93
	Out of the ordinary pressures	95
7	**Local radio, past, present and future**	**100**
	Origins	100
	Developments	102
	Competition	105
	The future and narrowcasting	106
8	**Life as a freelancer**	**109**
	Freelancing: the agonies and the ecstasies	109
	Developing your freelance work	113
	Case study	115
9	**Final thoughts**	**118**
	Advice and pointers	118
Resources and references		**123**
	Books	123
	Post-graduate journalism courses	123
	Useful websites	124
Appendix: NUJ Code of Conduct		**127**
Index		**128**

If you require a decent explanation of a political situation or a social issue, if you want to decide whether to spend money on tickets for film X, play Y or concert Z, the radio will help you, as it will with football scores, financial advice and little dream worlds.

The figures show it. Nine people in ten listen every day. We listen when we wake up, while we drive, iron, wallpaper, wash up, work on our computers. It is the friend in our head, the clock, the conscience and the cheerer-up. As competition has grown, television has thinned down. Radio has stayed alive by being varied, daring (and) original.

Gillian Reynolds

Acknowledgements

My heart-felt thanks to the following who have kindly answered my questions, offered advice and shared their professional expertise: Geoff Amos, Martin Ballard, Sonia Deol, Ed Doolan, Steve England, Lis Henderson, Ben Jackson, Liam McCarthy, Jennifer Norton, Alex Trelinski, Monica Winfield and Julian Worricker. Especial thanks to my old friend and colleague Tony Wadsworth whose example and support over many years finally determined me to take the plunge and make broadcasting a full-time occupation. I am very grateful to Stephen Woolfe who cast an expert eye over a draft of Chapter 5 and saved me from making a number of howlers, and to Stephen Butt who read a draft of Chapter 7 and offered helpful comments. Peter Liddle of the Leicestershire Museums' Arts and Records Service kindly allowed me to reproduce one of his press releases. My biggest debt of thanks is recorded in the dedication.

John Florance

I am delighted that John Florance has agreed to write this book. He is a rare breed in broadcasting; by that I mean he is one of those few broadcasters who has the ability to talk to the Prime Minister one day and an ordinary member of the public the next day. I first met John when I organised a Radio Conference at Loughborough College in the 1980s and he was confident, articulate and knowledgeable. I have listened to him many times on BBC Radio Leicester and on BBC Radio 2FM and BBC Radio 4FM. John Florance is a broadcaster who understands the industry well and can explain it to you. I have no hesitation in recommending this book to any aspiring broadcaster, whether you are in student radio, hospital radio or a new entrant to the world of professional broadcasting, this **book really can help you become a top broadcaster**. Read John Florance's work, learn from what he says and *you can* have a future in the industry.

Graham Lawlor
(aka '*Mr Educator*')

Introduction

One-minute summary – Radio broadcasting and DJ work are often thought to be jobs that require the same skills. They are not.

In this introduction, you will learn how to:

- ▶ develop your personal skills as a broadcaster
- ▶ increase your knowledge base as a broadcaster, so that you become more confident, more knowledgeable and a better broadcaster.

'This is John Florance. He works at Radio Leicester.'
'Oh . . . you're a DJ. How interesting.'

This conversation, or something like it, is a regular feature of my life and it never fails to cause irritation. There is a huge difference between being a DJ and being a presenter. This book is about the latter occupation and it's worthwhile spending some time teasing out the differences between it and the former.

The DJ's principal job is introducing discs. Put as baldly as that it sounds simple enough. But of course it's by no means easy. Apart from having considerable technical skills and expert knowledge, the DJ has also to make him or herself memorably different from all the other people doing a similar job in the area . . . or in the country at large if they are lucky enough to work on a national station.

This, in effect, means that the DJs don't just present programmes, they present *themselves.* That is, create an image or persona which produces that unique sound and flavour which will make people want to tune in and listen.

A radio presenter has also to present him or herself to some extent. But the job is rather more complex. Whilst the show may well contain music, this will not be the most important ingredient. The presenter's job is to create entertaining speech. This means she or he has to have something interesting and entertaining to say on whatever topics are current and be able to ask relevant and provoking questions so that they can get the most stimulating performance out of the guest or whoever is on the line during a phone-in sequence.

What a presenter needs

The presenter has to possess the following qualities, attributes and skills:

- quickness of thought
- brass neck
- good microphone voice
- good sense of humour
- excellent general/local knowledge
- good technical skills.

Quickness of thought

All programmes are live and so anything might happen. Chapter 6 will explore this more fully. At this point, suffice it to say that all programmes throw up topics, ideas, problems or talking points which were unforeseen. If a programme *doesn't* have its fair share of surprises it will probably sound dull and stale. A lively programme is a spontaneous programme and spontaneity takes quickness of thought and flexibility. This is not to say that planning isn't vital (something about which more is said in Chapter 2) but if you don't enjoy living dangerously some of the time you are on the air perhaps the job isn't for you. In particular, if your programme contains a general phone-in element (see Chapter 4) you will need all your resources of wit, knowledge and...

Brass neck

...which is a Midlands term meaning 'cheek' or 'nerve'. In this context it means having the confidence to utter opinions, some of which you'll only just have discovered you hold; argue, sometimes strongly, cases you don't personally hold (the Devil always needs an advocate) and generally have the cheek to believe that thousands of people are so interested in you and your guests that they'll tune in regularly to hear what you are up to. And as part of this attractive package you must have a...

Good microphone voice

...which is not necessarily the same thing as having a conventionally 'beautiful' voice. Actually, defining in the abstract what makes a good microphone voice is almost impossible. But you'll know one when you hear it. For our purposes, a good microphone voice is one which the audience enjoys listening to. I once asked a speech therapist about this and she said that the voices people enjoyed listening to suggested the presenters were *relaxed*. Their voices sound neither forced nor tired.

Above all, it must be a voice which creates *trust*. Over a single month I've had listeners call my programme worried about pensions and benefits; distressed at the prospect of going into hospital; concerned at moving into a retirement home; outraged at the service offered by a shop; disturbed at a sudden crisis of faith.

Such folk will only call if they think they can trust you, that you will listen sympathetically and attentively and perhaps be able to offer practical help. All they have to go on is your voice and what you say. If they don't like the sound of you, if they don't trust you, they won't bother to listen. And they certainly won't want to phone the programme to open up to you and everyone listening. Having said this, you won't be able to please all the people all of the time. Inevitably you will receive hate mail, a topic dealt with in Chapter 10.

Good sense of humour

In addition to all this, having a lively sense of humour is vital. Not just because listeners like to hear funny things, but because if you lack a sense of humour you will lack a sense of proportion . . . of knowing what is important and what is not and adjusting your presentation accordingly. It is depressing indeed to listen to several hours of ranting about the ills of the world, just as it's tiring to listen to several hours of levity.

Almost without thinking you've got to know what tone is suitable at that particular moment . . . when humour is needed to lighten things up and when a situation needs serious or dignified treatment. You can't take your eye off the ball!

Excellent general/local knowledge

All the qualities I've mentioned above are not ones you can easily acquire. They are mainly gifts and talents: either you've got them or you haven't. Of course, if you do possess them they can and must be honed, tutored and trained throughout your career. But a good general and local knowledge is something you can and must work at.

You must have a deep understanding of your patch. If you don't sound as if you know where your callers live, the problems those areas face and (very important for older listeners) what was there once but is no more (theatres, pubs, shops, fields etc.) you will never win wholehearted confidence.

You will need to keep up with current affairs and as many of the 101 other things that interest people as you can: sport, music, entertainment, television, the arts and so on. Admittedly it's difficult to keep abreast of everything and some things will interest you more than others. But if you have a blind spot about something which you know many listeners are interested in (eg. the doings of the local speedway team or the events of *Coronation Street*) make sure you *find out* what is going on.

You should have a natural curiosity about most things so you will be absorbing facts and details almost unconsciously on a daily basis. You'll never know when this material will come in handy. The great poet Alexander Pope wrote: 'A little knowledge is a dangerous thing'. In the wider scheme of things he was doubtless correct. But for the presenter a little knowledge about a great many things is an invaluable thing. You are a *broad*caster not a *narrow*caster, which means that your knowledge, expertise and range of interest must approach that of your potential audience.

Good technical skills

I've left this section till last but not because it is unimportant. Far from it. The skills needed to operate a mixing desk to produce the best possible sound is the minimum, most basic knowledge you will need. But what comes in addition to this, all the qualities and attributes I've briefly outlined above, are what will make you a good presenter. Any fool can learn how to operate a desk competently. I know because I don't find it easy to learn such skills. I have to work hard to acquire every new technique and I envy mightily my colleagues who can seemingly just look at a new bit of kit or computer program and just *use* it. But, to repeat, technical skills are just the start of it. Such skills are, as it were, *the stage on which you perform.* It's got to be there, but it's your performance to which audiences will be listening.

A final thought before we move on. I once asked a very experienced presenter what I should always keep in mind about the job. After a pause he said: 'Always remember that you're addressing an *individual* and not a mass meeting. And keep asking yourself "Why should that person want you in their home?"' If you can take to heart that first bit of advice and can answer that question clearly and honestly and constantly adjust your performance in the light of your answer, well, you might have a good career ahead of you.

Tutorial

1. What are the qualities needed by a good presenter?
2. What are the qualities of a good microphone voice?

Seminar discussion

'Good Radio involves the listener in a one-to-one intimate relationship.'

Do you agree with this statement?
If so, why?
If not, why not?

Practical assignments

1. Listen to a BBC station and an independent station in your area in the UK, or a public service and commercial radio station if you are outside the UK.
   a) Make a minute-by-minute analysis of what you hear. How does the presenter build his or her relationship with the listener?
   b) What are the main differences between public service and commercial radio broadcasting?

2. Conduct an internet search and find websites like *www.ukradio.com*

3. Research the issue of music copyright on internet radio, what are the implications for the future of radio on the net?

1

Starting Out

One-minute summary – The most commonly asked question from aspiring broadcasters, is 'how do you recommend I start?'

This is difficult because the industry has constantly changed and is changing all of the time. But there are things you can do.

In this chapter, you will learn:

- the two ways to become a top presenter
- how to listen and learn to improve your own radio
- how to analyse radio output and develop your own understanding
- how to gain valuable experience and develop your own broadcasting
- how you can emulate top radio broadcasters and become a major success.

The ways in

There are two ways of becoming a radio presenter: the unofficial and the official.

Actually, things aren't even as clear-cut as that. Most presenters are freelancers and there is no career structure and precious little training for the job. So, in effect, most presenters fall into the job almost by accident, or slide into it from a related occupation like journalism. Becoming a presenter is an indirect and sometimes perplexing process.

Even so, it still makes sense to talk about 'unofficial' and 'official' ways in.

By 'unofficial' I mean getting yourself known at a local station, gaining experience and skills and then, with luck, getting some sort of job.

By 'official' I mean going on a training course and applying for a job suitable to your qualifications. As we shall see, this generally involves taking a post-graduate diploma in radio journalism and then, having done a stint in a newsroom, easing yourself into a presenter's chair.

Even that course of action won't necessarily guarantee you a job. However, a qualification in radio journalism is an excellent thing to have. It puts you in a good position for gaining an 'in' to a radio station and once you *are* in you can work towards a job presenting. Moreover, the news skills you will gain on the course will help you a great deal when that all important opening comes or when you are able to create one for yourself.

Having said this, there are a number of ways in which you can gain valuable experience and thus help yourself and put you ahead of the game.

Listening and learning

It should go without saying that anyone with ambitions to pursue a career in radio should be passionate about the medium. That passion inevitably expresses itself in listening to a great deal of radio and being well informed about the industry.

I say that this should go without saying because I am genuinely surprised at the number of aspirant broadcasters I meet who actually listen to very little radio. To be fair, they generally tune in to their favourite one or two stations, and in particular to their favourite presenters. But to be well informed about the industry, and more importantly to learn about the ways in which programmes are constructed and presented, it is necessary to listen to as wide a range of stations and broadcasters as possible.

If you live in a city or an average sized town there will be no problem about finding stations on your dial. But wherever you live you should be able to listen to a reasonable range of programmes. As well as the BBC's five national networks there are BBC local stations, national independents like Classic FM and Virgin, local independents and incrementals as well as pirate stations.

Even if you dislike or are not interested in the kind of material put out by some of these it is always worth tuning in, if only for a few minutes, just to see what they are doing, what 'sound' they are promoting and how the presenters tailor their styles to that sound.

A radio enthusiast is a radio junkie! But if you really want to learn the skills and arts of radio presentation you should not listen *passively*. You have got to become an *active* listener.

What exactly does this mean? Here is an exercise to help you become an active listener.

Active listening

Find a station to which you don't ordinarily listen, preferably one which is predominantly speech-based. Tune in for about an hour and ideally record this so that you can listen again to check details and impressions. You will also need a watch or a clock.

As you listen, jot down an analysis of what you are hearing. This analysis will be of two kinds: objective and subjective.

Objective analysis

This consists of a note of timings and subject matter. You might produce something like this for an hour of listening.

10.00 News.

10.05 Travel news followed by presenter ident jingle.

10.06 Presenter gives 'menu' for next hour. Gives phone-in number and identifies station. Introduces disc.

10.08 Disc. Beatles *I Feel Fine*.

10.11 Presenter introduces studio guest . . . local council leader who in the previous week had announced the closure of a number of branch libraries and stirred up a storm because of this. During this session there are four calls from listeners who speak directly to guest. Presenter identifies station twice and announces phone-in number three times.

10.25 Interview ends and presenter introduces disc. Simon and Garfunkel *Bridge Over Troubled Waters.*

10.29 Station ident. Jingle. Presenter takes three general calls on the iniquity of the government; an old friend with whom the caller is attempting to re-establish contact; and why are they digging up the city centre again?

10.38 Presenter introduces traffic flash from local Area Traffic Control. There's been a bad accident on the local motorway which is causing tail-backs.

10.40 Trail and station ident jingle.

10.41 Presenter introduces an historian from the local university who's written a book on life on the home front during the Second World War. During the interview there are two calls from listeners about evacuees and one about rationing.

10.56 Disc Flanagan and Allan *Run Rabbit Run.*

These bare facts will enable you to deduce what kind of sound the station is aiming to create and the audience it is aiming itself at.

- Predominantly speech based.
- Subject matter and presenter's manner indicate that the audience is mainly middle aged.
- Discs 'punctuate' the speech rather than the other way around.
- Two of the discs also indicate the nature of the target audience.
- The final disc clearly chosen to link with previous item but it could indicate an appeal to an older audience.
- It's an 'access' station with calls taken throughout the sequence.

Subjective analysis

This will depend largely on your perception of the style the presenter is adopting.

As a result of listening to the sequence you might jot down a set of notes like this.

The presenter sounds as if he is in his 40s and has a friendly and involving manner. He is not aggressive and abrasive but when talking to the local politician he asked provoking questions indicating that he was well informed and on the side of listeners. Callers mostly sounded as though they were retired. Three were clearly talking about the war from first hand experience. Two of them sounded like young mums. The presenter was able to deal well with all age groups but sounded a bit impatient with one rambling caller. He was careful to let callers make their points and then cut them off politely. The pace was kept up but it didn't sound 'breathless'. Jingles and idents sounded 'mellow' rather than aggressive. Presenter had clearly done more than just glance at the book under discussion. Asked specific, informed questions aimed at getting the guest to prompt memories. This could have been simply nostalgic but was also informative. All in all, an involving listen if you like this style of broadcasting.

The object of such an exercise is to get you to think about:

- What the station is attempting to do.
- Whether it is achieving its objective.
- How the presenter tailors his/her performance to that of the station's audience.

Do this exercise for a number of stations with differing styles and content. After you've done this a few times you will find yourself registering all sorts of things about a presenter's style almost without being consciously aware of the fact. This will assist you in picking up techniques, skills and tips to help you in your time behind the microphone.

To sum up:

- Listen regularly to a range of radio stations and presenters.
- Listen attentively and critically.
- Apply what you have learnt.

Gaining experience

Exercises like the one described above will give you a vital sense of how radio programmes and sequences are constructed and something of the range of styles of presentation there are. But how can the lessons you have learned be applied?

The more practical experience of broadcasting you can gain the better you will be placed to be appointed to a position in mainstream radio or be successful in applying for training courses.

At this point, a word of caution is advisable. Gaining this experience is, these days, far from easy. You will need tenacity and enthusiasm to succeed!

Broadly, there are two ways of gaining experience:

- Work experience at your local station.
- Involving yourself in hospital and/or campus radio.

There was a time when getting into a local station was relatively (and I stress the word *relatively*) easy. Ten years ago when staff had more time than they do now, sympathetic broadcasters, especially in BBC stations, would sometimes take aspirants under their wings and teach them the 'basics': how to use the equipment, mix packages, do reports and vox pops etc. etc.

I know of a number of broadcasters who got started in just this way. Indeed it was how I got started in the industry well over twenty years ago. I appeared as a guest on a programme, the producer liked what I did and gradually I got 'absorbed' into the station, learning as I went.

However, this rarely happens these days because staff are a lot busier now and because this sort of 'back-door' training is frowned upon. Even so, it's still worth writing to your local station.

Write a succinct letter direct to the editor or manager. You should know the out-put of the station, explain that you want experience and try to present as truthful and enthusiastic account of your ambitions as you can. You just might be lucky.

If, of course, you know, however remotely, someone who works at a radio station, make use of them! Try to persuade them to show you round and give you the benefit of their experience and if possible give you some training.

Gaining an 'in' to a hospital radio station is, perhaps, slightly easier – but it's still difficult. Every hospital of any size has a radio station generally broadcast by cable. Some of them are very professional indeed. Steve England has been involved in the running of Hospital Radio Fox at the Leicester Royal Infirmary since the station was established in the mid-eighties. I asked him about what opportunities there are in hospital radio. Here is what he said.

> In my time hospital broadcasting has grown hugely and become considerably more professional. There is a national umbrella organisation – the Hospital Broadcasting Association, formerly the National Association of Hospital Broadcasting Organisations – which is the voice of the movement. It holds regular conferences and keeps us all in touch with developments.
>
> Different hospital radio stations run their recruitment schemes in different ways, but ours is not unusual.
>
> We get two or three applications a week from people who want to work at the station. Most write direct to the hospital and ask for their letter of enquiry to be passed on to us. We're looking for real commitment so we have regular 'New Members' Meetings'. A number of those whom have contacted us are invited along and we make it clear what is expected of anyone who we invite to join the team. For a start, we're a charity. We get no financial help and we have to raise all our money ourselves. So being involved in that side of things is vital. We also expect volunteers to take an active interest in all aspects of the station – we're not just looking for star presenters! A hospital radio station, like every other station has engineers, programme producers, music librarians, sports commentators, administrators and so on.
>
> We also have a side to our work found nowhere else. We actually go out and meet our captive audience! Our volunteers visit the wards on a regular basis and collect requests, for instance.
>
> If, having been told all this and a lot more, they still seem keen then they will be asked back for a comprehensive tour of the station. We might even ask for references before someone is

asked back. We have to deter time-wasters and, to repeat, we need people who show real enthusiasm for and commitment to the station. If you do demonstrate those qualities we will try to take you on for a probationary period and give you proper training for three months.

I know this sounds a bit forbidding, but it is important that people know what to expect... and if you do make it over those first hurdles there is a lot of fun and satisfaction to be had in hospital radio!

Involving yourself in campus radio is perhaps the easiest way of gaining experience, always assuming that you have gained a university place.

Most universities have some sort of radio operation. These vary in quality enormously but at their best they are very professional sounding indeed. Expressing an interest and getting yourself involved in the campus station shouldn't be that difficult. Introduce yourself and make yourself indispensable without being predictable and boring.

If you can get yourself involved in any of these kinds of broadcasting try, if at all possible, to gain experience in as many departments as possible, even if it's just as an observer. See how programmes are produced; how packages are mixed; how radio journalists operate; how programmes, especially outside broadcasts, are engineered etc. You should aim to glean as much knowledge as possible.

If you can, try to make a show reel, a cassette demonstrating your style of presentation. If you can afford it, have this made at a recording studio with professional help. You will have to mock up a programme segment containing interviews, discs, jingles etc. This will take preparation, the cooperation of potential interviewees (you can always use sensible friends) and so on. But being able to present a station with a decently put together show reel which demonstrates your abilities will put you a nose ahead of the field.

At this point it is instructive to hear from two freelance presenters whose careers illustrate the range of ways in which access to the industry can be gained and how careers develop.

Case studies

Julian Worricker

Julian Worricker is the much respected co-presenter of Radio 5 Live's Breakfast Show.

Like most people he became a presenter in a rather indirect way, although his career is mainly an example of the 'official' route into presentation. When I asked him about his radio career this is what he said.

> When I was at school I helped out at a small hospital radio in a huge Victorian psychiatric hospital. I was never allowed on-air, and frankly I didn't get the impression that many people were listening. Although I've always been an enthusiastic radio listener I didn't think about radio again until my final year at Leicester University. I read English and have always been interested in current affairs and I decided I wanted to be a journalist. I applied for a number of postgraduate courses and ended up on a radio journalism course at Falmouth.
>
> That course prepared me for not making a complete fool of myself in the newsroom. I got some freelance shifts in Devon which was useful experience. Then a full time job at BBC Radio Leicester.
>
> This was in the mid-eighties and the newsroom was full of very experienced journalists so initially it was a bit intimidating because they really knew the patch very well. Again, I learnt an awful lot over three years. I then did a stint as presenter/reporter on *Midlands Today*, the local TV news programme. But radio was my first love and I moved back to Radio Leicester after six months, this time as News Editor.
>
> During this time I went on a BBC presentation course, rarer then than now! I was twinned with a friend and former colleague Sue McGarry and the trainer liked our joint style and chemistry. So when I began to feel frustrated at not doing enough real broadcasting as a News Editor I began to think about doing some more presentation. I'd filled in for one or two presenters when they were ill and enjoyed the experience.

When the old Radio 5 started Sue and I luckily got the job of presenting the drive-time sequence from Manchester. So I threw away my BBC staff number, the pension disappeared and I did that programme for three happy years.

When Radio 5 bit the dust I freelanced for a bit which allowed me to network and establish contacts. Very important that! When 5 Live started I did various bits of presentation and reporting. I did the weekend breakfast programme for a time and then drive-time for a year. Then I was lucky enough to be twinned with Victoria Derbyshire on the breakfast programme which I have been doing ever since.

What advice would I give to aspiring presenters? Listen to as many stations as you can. That is vital! But my own career demonstrates that luck, being in the right place at the right time and knowing the right people play a big part, as they do in any career, of course. This is not to denigrate the acquiring of experience and skills and having a feel for the medium, a good voice and all the rest of it. These are absolutely essential. But I can't help thinking that most presenters have been very lucky in their careers.

Sonia Deol

Sonia Deol is the bubbly host of BBC 2's Network East programme and is a presenter at BBC London Live. Known as 'the Asian Zoe Ball' she has made a career for herself through energy and ambition. She has undergone little formal training and her progress makes an interesting contrast with Julian's.

I've been a radio enthusiast since I was about eight. I remember making pretend radio programmes with a tape recorder in my bedroom. My guests were long-suffering family and friends. I've never deviated from my ambition to work in the media and I've always wanted to be a talk-show presenter, not a DJ.

When I was 14 the first Comic Relief was launched and I saw this as a way of getting on air. I phoned BBC Radio WM and said I wanted to co-present a programme and I'd get sponsorship for the number of words I spoke on air. There wasn't much encouragement but I took sponsorship forms to school, kept on phoning the station and when I told them how much sponsorship I'd got they miraculously agreed to let me loose behind a microphone.

I remember going to the studios at Pebble Mill for the first time and thinking, 'One day I'll work here!' I had no doubts.

Anyway, that first broadcast was awful. I was terribly nervous and thank goodness I've lost the tape. But I wasn't discouraged and when I was 16 I worked on a community station during the summer holidays. I did discussions on all the usual stuff, arranged marriages, women's problems, multiculturalism and all the rest of it. At that age, heaven knows what the listeners made of me! But it was a great learning experience.

Next I went to the University of Hertfordshire where I read Humanities. During the vacations I managed to wangle a job at the now defunct TV Asia. I worked as a continuity announcer and then, after much pushing, as a regular reporter, finally on the Breakfast Show.

When I was 21 I applied for a job at Sunrise Radio, broadcasting to London and the Home Counties. I sent my CV and a show-reel and badgered them by phone to give me an interview. They relented and at the interview I bombarded the editor with programme ideas – I kept a note-book and jotted these down as I thought of them. He gave in and I was taken on to do the late evening show. As I was still at university this suited me fine. Later I did stints on all the main sequences and this taught me about how different times of day demand different presentational styles.

After this, I worked at Radio XL in Birmingham which was then just starting. I was taken on as mid-morning presenter and head of production. This involved scripting and producing commercials and training staff to use the equipment as well as presenting. As you can imagine it was all wonderful experience because I had to master so many valuable skills.

I did nine months at XL, then rejoined Sunrise before finally joining the Asian Network in Leicester and now I'm happily employed at BBC London Live. I also present TV programmes and I like to pick 'n' mix, though radio is my first and abiding love.

The recipe for getting on? Well, you can't underestimate the power of self-belief and confidence. Never take no for an answer! You've got to sell yourself at job interviews and be yourself on air.

Tutorial

1. What is active listening?
2. What experience opportunities exist in your local hospital radio station or student radio station?

Seminar discussion

Radio broadcasting involves presenting a part of yourself to the audience. The top radio broadcasters read avidly and can comment on any particular aspect of popular culture.

a) How well do you understand popular culture and current affairs?

b) Who is your local MP or local representative?

c) Who is the local councillor for your area?

d) Who is the top regional broadcaster in your area and why?

e) Why is the BBC Radio 2FM afternoon programme, *Steve Wright in the Afternoon* the market leader in UK Radio?

Practical assignments

1. A local radio afternoon programme was cancelled. The young presenter, a freelancer, lost his job. He had local school students recording sketches they had written to broadcast as they put it, 'like *Steve Wright in the Afternoon*'.

   (a) Write down a half page analysis of why this radio station cancelled the programme.

   (b) What should the strengths of local radio be?

2. Buy your local paper and look for 10 items of local information. Use these items of information to build links into an imaginary radio programme, making them interesting, informative or funny.

3. Top radio broadcasters have unique selling points (USPs). Their personality is the commodity their audience 'buys' by listening to the programme.
   List 10 positive aspects of your personality that people find interesting. These are your USPs. What are your top three USPs that make you different from other broadcasters?

4. Identify 10 magazines, newspapers or periodicals that you can start reading today, to improve your knowledge of popular culture and current affairs.

2

How to Conduct an Interview

One-minute summary – Interviewing is the bedrock of broadcasting. A good interview technique is essential if you are to make it as a good broadcaster.

In this chapter you will learn:

- how to ask the right questions to bring out the best in your interviewee
- how to follow the guidelines that will create great radio and turn you into a top broadcaster
- how to conduct a soft interview that will make a local event shine with interest.

There are no golden rules

Conducting a good, entertaining, informative interview is no easy matter. It is certainly not a question of simply applying a number of well-tried techniques which will inevitably result in a lively performance by the person being questioned.

The reason for this is simple. An interview is a form of human interaction. Because human beings are not machines, a technique or kind of question which works for one person won't necessarily work for someone else. In fact, gaining a good interview is, in all sorts of ways, a rather mysterious business.

Time and again I've found myself looking forward to interviewing someone because, on the face of it, they are interesting in themselves or have a good story to tell, only to find that on the day what emerged was far from being sparkling. There might have been a number of reasons for this. Perhaps they were not feeling well, they were in a bad mood or were reluctant to talk for a number of reasons. Or perhaps *I* got off on the wrong foot with them. There is no law to say that people must immediately like each other or establish mutual rapport, let alone respect.

But equally I've often found that what looks on paper to be an unpromising interview turns into gold. Almost invariably this is because the interviewee has the kind of 'big' and attractive personality which can transform the most unpromising subject into something warm and compelling. For example, I have often found that funeral directors make excellent interviewees! On the face of it, death and funeral arrangements hardly make for riveting radio. Potentially, they are singularly depressing subjects. But funeral directors have to have deep sympathies. They understand people. And part of this understanding seems to be that of making their job interesting for the rest of us. Often their stories have a kind of black humour. But in all the interviews I've done with funeral directors no listener has ever called in to complain about bad taste or irreverence. Quite the reverse. We have often received calls saying how enjoyable the interview was.

My point is that even an interview about a forthcoming fete or garden party can be transformed into something interesting if the interviewee is able to speak about it with quirky enthusiasm.

Now, not everyone can do that. But at least you, the interviewer, can provide the situation and context in which that is more likely to happen. It is your job to ask questions which will bring out the best in your interviewee.

There are no golden rules about doing this. As in so much of broadcasting, you have got to find your own way because you are a unique personality and so will have a unique impact on those who appear in your studio.

Even so, there are a number of guide-lines which can prove invaluable and which will, after time become second nature to you. Let's look at them now.

What kind of interview?

In my experience, aspirant speech radio presenters have the idea that they will spend their time on air talking to powerful and influential men and women: MPs, captains of industry, academic experts and the like. They are would-be Jeremy Paxmans and Kirsty Warks. Disabuse yourself of this right away!

You *will* of course, speak to such people occasionally. But an awful lot of your time will probably be taken up with interviewing people who want to publicise events, get a charity's message across, talk about a book they've written, announce the results of a wild-life survey, and so on.

Any programme will contain a range of different kinds of interview. Each will demand a different approach. And so the first thing you have to do when preparing for an interview is to decide what *kind* of interview this one will be.

Soft and hard

Traditionally, interviews have been divided into two categories: the *soft* and the *hard*.

What do we mean by these terms?

Hard interviews are generally with politicians and decision makers. In other words, the powerful men and women whose actions need public scrutiny. Interviewing them is, in a sense, part of the democratic process because it is important for them to be accountable to the electorate. The interviewer is insisting that they defend their actions and decisions because such actions and decisions affect the lives of the rest of us.

The hard interview is, then, a kind of *interrogation*.

Because dealing with public figures is a specialised and very important skill the whole of the next chapter is devoted to this subject.

If the hard interview is interrogative, the soft interview is more a kind of conversation. The object is to get the best out of an interviewee by being informal and encouraging them to talk naturally. In a hard interview you challenge; in a soft interview you prompt.

Of course, these categories are not water-tight. During a hard interview you may well ask soft questions and *vice versa*. And if an interview goes off in an unexpected direction you may have to be prepared to change the tone of your questioning, something I will discuss below. But as a rough and ready guide here are the attributes of soft and hard interviews.

SOFT	HARD
Informal	Formal
Conversational	Challenging
Light	Heavy
Questions which prompt	Questions fuelled by information and fact

In the next chapter I will deal with how to prepare for hard interviews. But even soft ones demand proper preparation. A subject we will look at now.

The importance of preparation

Not long ago I interviewed the author of one of the self-help books which are so popular these days. It was the kind of volume which claims it can help you achieve your ambitions and create the success you want. The book was no worse than many of its kind, but as with so many it over-states its case. One chapter is called 'Plan, Plan, Plan'. The burden of this is that you should leave absolutely nothing to chance.

Spontaneity

Well, in many circumstances I dare say this is admirable advice. But in live broadcasting you cannot plan for every eventuality, and even if you could it would be a bad thing because the life of live broadcasting lies in its spontaneity.

And if we turn to interviewing, the very heart of live talk radio, spontaneity is of the essence. The best interviews have a life of their own and take off in quite unexpected ways if a rapport or chemistry is established. By definition this is the sort of thing for which planning is impossible. The interviewer must, paradoxically, be prepared for the unexpected and allow things to develop in unforeseen ways. This is what makes for exciting broadcasting. Simply working down a list of prepared questions is both lazy and boring.

Preparation

However, this is far from saying that preparing for an interview is unimportant. You cannot frame intelligent questions without knowing something of the subject of the interview. Moreover, if you persist in asking dumb and uninformed questions your interviewee is probably going to feel antagonised if not insulted and so will not give of his or her best.

But be warned, there is a paradox about this! I find that the more I know about a subject the more difficult it is to 'ground' an interview. By this I mean that any successful interview must be conducted in terms which listeners must understand. In this sense you, the interviewer, have got to ask the kind of questions which they might ask if they were given the opportunity.

You need to know enough to ask relevant questions, but if you know a great deal about the subject of an interview (bus routes, nuclear power, gardening, modern drama, Gilbert and Sullivan, savings plans, computers etc., etc.), you must make every effort not to show off your knowledge or ask questions simply to impress your interviewee. This gives the impression that you are conducting a private conversation which excludes the listener.

Questioning is a subject we shall return to in this chapter. Meanwhile, it is worth repeating the guide-line that you should always know enough to ask the right questions – the questions to which the listeners want to know the answers.

Cues

Cue writing is a basic skill. The cue is the introduction to an interview. It is generally scripted and it has three main functions, though it might not be appropriate for each individual cue to use all of them. These functions are:

- to tease
- to provide context
- to introduce.

Teasing

This simply means stimulating the listener to want to hear further. A cue often (but not always) starts with a tease in the form of a question.

Here are a few examples.

> When is a building an eyesore and when is it a valuable piece of built heritage? Bywater Hall seems to be both judging from the row which has erupted since its possible demolition was announced two weeks ago.

> Each time you visit an internet site or e-mail someone you leave a trail of information behind you. Where does it go? Should you worry about it?

> Are you retired? And if so, are you at a loose end? If so, our next guest may well have some useful suggestions for you.

> Exactly fifty years ago today pupils at a local school set out on an expedition which passed into legend.

Contextualising

No interview takes place in a vacuum. The listener needs information to allow him or her to understand what is being said properly. So the cue usually provides facts, figures, statistics etc to allow the interview to proceed without the laborious extraction from the interviewee of large quantities of information.

The danger, however, is of providing *too much* in the way of context. If you do this, you may well have done much of the interviewee's job yourself. Your aim should be to provide just enough basic information to allow the person being interviewed to answer your questions clearly and to provide more information if this is relevant.

Let us now add contextualising material to our four cues.

> Bywater Hall was built in the 1890s and, according to the local civic society and other conservation groups, it's a unique example of late Victorian provincial architecture. But it has been boarded up for 12 years and is, according to the local authority, in a dangerous state.

> Research just out indicates that internet users are more and more concerned to protect their privacy . . . and on this

programme the number of calls expressing concern about the personal information stored on computers has increased greatly.

Our local Age Concern Office has just compiled a directory of organisations and agencies which are looking for volunteers with work experience to work in a wide range capacities.

If you were at Kendal Rise School in 1951 you are bound to recall a trip which caught the national headlines. In those austere days a trip abroad was very unusual for ordinary folk. But when that trip was to Spain by double-decker bus... well, that caught the imagination of people across the country.

Introducing

The third function of the cue is to introduce the interviewee or interviewees. Usually this is simply done with a name and occupation or a brief explanation of their interest in the matter in hand. So our four notional cues might conclude like this.

John Eliot is the Chair of the local civic society . . . he thinks it would be an act of vandalism if the hall came down. Ron Atkins is from the local authority planning department and he has a different view.

To address some of these concerns we are joined by Mike Curtis from the Data Commission Office . . . the body charged with applying the law relating to computers. And Lisa Johnston of the pressure group POP, which stands for Protect Our Privacy.

The directory is a surprisingly comprehensive one, and the person who put in the time compiling it is with us now. She is Anne French.

Kendal Rise School is, of course, still going and on Saturday it plays host to a reunion of those who went on the trip. Its organiser, and someone who remembers it well, is Ken Simpson.

I am not saying that these cues are other than functional, and I am certainly not providing them as patterns to be slavishly copied. But they do their job. They are reasonably brief, to the point and allow interviewers and interviewees to get on with the job in hand having cleared the 'basics' out of the way.

At this point it should be said that different programmes go about cue production in different ways. I know of some where the producer or researcher do all the cue writing. For two reasons I do not think this is a good idea.

Writing the cue

Firstly, if *you* have to write the cue, you have to get the research which underpins the interview into your head. So cue writing is an excellent discipline for preparing comprehensively for an interview.

Secondly, everyone has their own personal style of writing. You are the presenter, you have ownership of the programme so the cue, like everything else, should sound as if it belongs to you. If you write the cue, you will sound more natural reading it. If you read something that someone else has written, there will in all likelihood be a mismatch between the way you usually speak and the way it is written.

Having said that, a cue should not be used for over-indulging yourself. Cues should be relatively neutral and should certainly be to the point and crisp. They should not go on for longer than a minute and in general a well-written and informative cue can be delivered in 30–45 seconds.

Non scripted elements also help give a cue individuality and character. Two old stand-bys are appropriate music and the *vox pop*.

Music

The first cue, for example, could be introduced with a few bars of *This Old House*. Tuning round to a variety of stations in the past few days I've heard an item on fear of flying introduced by *Fly Me to the Moon*, one on recycling garments by *Second Hand Rose* and another on betting by *Luck be a Lady Tonight*. You see the problem already, I dare say! 'Appropriate' music can simply be clichéd music.

Music should be used sparingly and with thought.

Vox pop

The same applies to the *vox pop* – a sequence of 'sound bites' from members of the public on the subject in hand.

The first cue, again, might benefit from a *vox pop* especially if a variety of opinions are expressed. But *vox pops* need careful crafting. They should be crisply edited and not outstay their welcome. Incoherent remarks of the 'Well, I don't know really...' type have no place in a *vox pop*. A good *vox pop* takes time to produce and you may not have that time.

Nevertheless, used appropriately they can add another dimension to the introduction of certain interviews.

Finally, cues are generally scripted in advance. But of course in a lively programme you'll often have to introduce guests 'cold' because they've been booked whilst the programme has been on air in response to an evolving story. Unless you are a genius you won't be able to improvise a well-rounded paragraph of faultless prose to act as a cue. However, you *should* be able to introduce your guest with some context on the subject under discussion without a written script. An improvised cue might sound a bit rough around the edges, but that's all part of live broadcasting.

Researching an interview

I remarked above that cue writing is an important discipline because it ensures you research an interview adequately. How is such research done?

If you are lucky and have a team working on the programme (a producer and/or researcher, perhaps) then they will provide you with information. But frequently you are going to have to do the work yourself.

Stories and topics which might provide good interviews will originate in a variety of ways. Often you will be speaking to local people the programme has contacted, who can give a local spin to a national story. Or you will be speaking to people who have made local news. Your background information in such cases will come from newspapers, your station's newsroom and, perhaps, the internet.

But equally, interviews will come about as a result of contact made with the programme by people and organisations who write, phone or send in a press release.

Whether you like it or not, a good proportion of the interviews you do will be on the basis of a single sheet of A4 which tries to convince you that here is a topic worth following up.

It hardly needs saying that some press releases are better than others. The best stimulate curiosity in clearly written prose which set out the bare bones of a story. The worst ramble on for pages, full of irrelevant detail, often leaving you none the wiser at the end than at the beginning.

But if the writer has done his or her job properly, and providing the topic is reasonably uncontentious, it should be quite possible to write a cue and get a decent interview on the basis of a press release.

Even so, when you or a member of the programme team are contacting a prospective interviewee, *always* speak to that person to ensure that the topic in question is properly understood. Time spent in this way is never wasted and may suggest further fruitful areas of question.

Exercise

Look at the press release overleaf and write a cue for an interview with the curator of the Manor House, Peter Liddle. You don't need to stick to the pattern suggested above, but your cue should be crisp and include the three elements discussed above. To ensure that your prose is readable, read it out loud at a natural pace and make alterations if you find words and sentences difficult to get your tongue round.

Putting the interviewee at ease

I still remember my first radio appearance. I was then a teacher and a colleague had been engaged to present a series of evening programmes during the run up to the exam season. The idea was that O level literature candidates could call the station, ask questions about their set texts and a number of teachers assembled in the studio would mull over these questions in a way which would help revision.

Leicestershire Museums
Arts & Records Service
Leicestershire County Council
Museums, Arts and Records Service
BRINGING THE PAST TO LIFE
A celebration of Leicestershire Archaeology
On NATIONAL ARCHAEOLOGY DAY
Saturday 22nd July
Donington Le Heath Manor House
Events include:
➢ Crafts to see and try
➢ The Rare Breeds show
➢ Food from the past
➢ Re-enactment groups
➢ Archaeological detective agency
➢ Guided tours
➢ Games from the past
Wherever possible events are 'hands on'
Something for all the family!
ADMISSION FREE
Donington Le Heath Manor House is a 13th and 17th century stone house standing in 17th century gardens on the south-west edge of Coalville near Hugglescote. It is open 7 days a week from 11am – 5pm.
The Old Barn Restaurant is open 7 days a week in both the day and the evening
OTHER EVENTS AT DONINGTON
August 19th – 20th Donington in the English Civil War
September 16th Medieval Mayhem
October 22nd Life in the 13th Century Manor
November 19th 5000 Years of Death and Burial
December 9th Christmas at The Manor

I thought this sounded like a good idea and readily accepted when my colleague asked if I would like to join the team.

Nerves

As the fateful day approached I found myself getting more and more nervous at the prospect of broadcasting to thousands of listeners. In retrospect, I suspect that only a handful of youngsters tuned in. But at the time it felt as though the nation would be hanging on my every word.

As I waited for the bus to take me to the studio my nerves overtook me and it was all I could do to prevent myself from scurrying back to my bed-sit and phoning in to say I was sick . . . which in a sense I was – I felt nauseous with worry.

Anyway, I made it into the station and was ushered into the studio. It was the first time I'd ever been into one. In spite of my nerves I must have stammered out something coherent during that half hour because they invited me back the following week.

I was bitten by the radio bug and so a great career started! But I try to recapture that vivid sense of initiation anxiety every time I go on air because hardly a week, sometimes a day, goes past without my having to interview someone who is sitting in a radio studio for the first time. *You* might be an old hand, being on the air old hat. But to the broadcasting virgin simply being in a studio can be nerve-racking in the extreme. It follows that if you are to get the most out of your interviewees you must put them at their ease.

Reception

This is a team job and the process, ideally, should begin the moment a guest arrives at the station and is welcomed by the receptionist. The producer or p.a. on the programme may well be busy. Nevertheless, it is a vital part of his or her job to talk to interviewees, explain what is going on and what sort of questions they might expect. The object should be to ease the guest into the interview with as little fuss as possible. The presenter may only have the length of a commercial, trail or public service announcement to establish rapport with your guest. But a smile, a few words of encouragement and giving the impression of being relaxed and in control will help matters greatly.

If you have longer (for example, if you are playing a disc) you will have time to chat, explain what you'll be asking and generally using your charm to put your guest at ease.

It is extremely easy to become blasé, but do try to recall your 'first time' and how it felt. If you can do this you will develop a natural sympathy for your guests and develop, almost unconsciously, ways of making them feel relaxed and so able to give of their best.

If you find that 'first timers' often say at the end of the interview that you made it very easy for them you will have been doing your job properly in bringing out the best in your guest.

To sum up:

- smile
- talk to your guest off mic.
- explain what's going on
- tell him/her what questions to expect
- maintain an impression of relaxation.

Down the line/phone interviews

For most of the interviews you do your guest or guests will be sitting across the microphone from you. But interviews conducted by phone or on an ISDN line focus on an aspect of interviewing skills we haven't so far looked at.

Because guests interviewed like this can't see you and you can't see them an important part of human interaction is denied both parties. This is the non-verbal element in communication.

Body language

Whenever you talk to anyone you are, of course, listening to their words. But you are also, probably unconsciously, registering their body language. The way they hold their posture, the expression on their face, the movements of their arms and hands are all part of non-verbal communication. In a formal studio interview you will consciously use body language to reassure a nervous interviewee by nodding, smiling, holding friendly eye contact and by generally looking relaxed.

Equally, you will be observing your guest and registering their body language. You should be able to see when a guest is confident or nervous or in need of help not just through what they say but by the way they look. And you can often tell when a guest is about to end a point or an answer simply from the way they are sitting or from the expression on their face. (This isn't *always* the case, however. Some people have a body language quite at odds with what they are saying and this can be disconcerting!)

And of course you can signal by your expression and tone when an interview needs to come to an end.

All of this is common sense: body language and its interpretation is going on all the time whenever two or three are gathered together. But in the studio you can use it rather more consciously than you would in an informal meeting with friends. Remember, interviewing is a performance.

Tone of voice

If you can't see the interviewee this source of information and communication is denied you and this can make down-the-line interviews difficult. For example, I've found myself frequently surprised when a guest has suddenly ended an answer unexpectedly leaving me slightly floundering for a question. If I had been able to see him or her the situation would probably not have arisen because I'd have been able to read the body language.

So you must be unusually attentive to tone of voice in an unseen guest. Take as much time as you can before the interview to talk to them on pre-fade and explain what is going to happen, especially if they are nervous. Remember, if you find it difficult or uncomfortable to 'read' a guest because they are in a remote studio, they might be feeling as uneasy about you!

Questions

Broadly speaking there are two types of question: the 'open' and the 'closed'. A closed question will often lead to a one word ('yes' or 'no') or a very short answer. An open question encourages the interviewee to speak at length.

Examples of closed questions might be:

- Are you happy in your work?
- How old are you?
- Is it easy being a bricklayer and a housewife?
- When is the baby due?

A confident interviewee will, of course, treat questions like this as a cue to expand on their views or provide more information. And if you are confident in that confidence and are sure that such questions will achieve a good interview, then use them. But in general you should think in terms of 'open' questions.

Examples of open questions might be:

- How did you feel when you had finished the marathon?
- What exactly does the job entail?
- Why on earth did you do that?
- What drives you on?

Questions beginning with 'how', 'what', 'why' will almost certainly encourage your guest to 'flower' and enlarge upon his or her ideas.

Before we embark on a discussion of how an interview might be conducted, a word on preparing questions in advance.

Most presenters see thinking about questions as an integral part of the preparation process. So they append to the cues they write a series of questions or memory joggers for questions.

Here is list of questions you might devise for our first cue.

John
- Why is Bywater Hall so important in your opinion?
- But why should we preserve something which no longer has a use?
- You don't deny it's dangerous.

Ron
- The Civic Society says that to demolish the hall would be an act of vandalism. What do you say?
- How was it allowed to fall into disrepair in the first place?

- In what way is it dangerous?
- Have you tried to find a use for it?

Exercise

Write a list of 5 or 6 questions for the remaining three cues above. Make them relevant, short and don't be afraid to ask the obvious!

____

____

____

____

____

____

A word of warning here. If you simply work down the list of questions you'll probably end up with a perfectly satisfactory interview in that various relevant points will be expressed. But equally probably the interview will sound a trifle boring and predictable.

The best interviews take on a life of their own and the presenter must be flexible and spontaneous. Each of the interviewees might make a point which takes things off in an unexpected and interesting direction. Then you will have to scrap your carefully prepared questions, let the other interviewee respond and generally allow the two to argue it out. When this happens you become a kind of referee. It is then your job to see fair play, keep things relevantly on track and ensure that each has their say. You can always come back to your questions, if you think they haven't been covered, later on.

It's also worth saying that although you may write questions in one way, you'll probably ask them in another. In some circumstances firing crisp questions at an interviewee is the right thing to do. But in a soft interview the proceedings will usually be conversational rather than confrontational. You will probably ask questions in a more informal way than you have written them.

Above all, listen to what your guest says. Pick up on points that they make. Ask for clarification or a development of what they say. Listen out for comments that might take you off in fresh directions. There is, in a good interview, a sense of to and fro and give and take.

In spite of this, and in spite of the fact that you may well find yourself junking or reordering your prepared questions, it is important that you *do* prepare them. The very act of writing down a few questions helps you come to terms with the subject in hand and is an important part of the discipline of being a properly prepared interviewer.

'Bread and butter' interviews

At least some of the time you will be talking to people about events and subjects which are far from earth shattering: fetes, carnivals, charitable appeals, meetings and the like. These might be 'bread and butter' interviews but they will be a vital part of your station's commitment to the community it serves. A local station which doesn't reflect what is going on around the parish pump is not a *local* station.

Your job in of most of these interviews will be extracting information about where the event is taking place, what will be going on, when it starts, and so on. This, potentially, is pretty mundane and often your guest will be nervous because she or he hasn't been on air before. So, work hard at putting the guest at ease and always try to think of ways of making the event sound just a bit out of the ordinary. Preparation is doubly important here. Make sure you've got hold of all the facts. It's an opportunity lost if you only discover after the interview is over that a fete is being opened by an Olympic athlete or that camel rides are on offer.

Also, try to get beyond the facts of the case. Ask about the organisation of the event, how difficult it was to get people involved (this can lead on to a discussion of community spirit, or lack of it), how money raised will be spent and anything else you can think of to turn an event into an *event*!

Talking books

Writers, whether of fact or fiction, are always keen to get onto the radio. Or at least their publishers and agents are keen for them to get such exposure.

Most talk programmes have some sort of a policy to prevent the air waves being monopolised by authors attempting to flog their latest volume. For example, on the programme which I present we have three rules.

1. Any book has got to earn its place i.e. it or its author must be intrinsically interesting.

2. Novels don't earn a place unless they are written by a star writer of whom most people will have heard (Jeffrey Archer, J K Rowling etc) or by a local author.

3. Non-fiction books are considered if they are reputable. But we may set up an interview with an author of a book which seems to be barking (*Does God Live on Jupiter?*, *How Tea is Destroying Morality*, *How to Live to be 100 on 20 Fags a Day* etc) if we think we can have some fun with it.

These are flexible rules and I mention them not for others to follow but because I do think it is important that you do have some kind of policy towards the printed word.

But once you have decided you are going to interview an author it is important that you do him or her the courtesy of at least skimming through the book. One of the reasons why it's important to put books through a screening process is that if your programme is clogged with them you will have no time to give their books proper attention. And you cannot do a decent interview unless you know at least enough about the book to ask relevant questions.

So, with non-fiction books read the Introduction and skim read what look to be important chapters. Pick up on specific points in the text and ask questions about them. Try to get the *feel* of the book.

Fiction

Fiction is rather more difficult. The cliché question to ask of a novelist is, 'Tell me what it's about.' This gets you off to a bad start because it seems to indicate to your guest that you haven't even opened the book. You should include in your cue at least something of the book's subject matter – a taste of the book's story. So, although you probably won't have time to read the whole book, again you must have read enough to get a real flavour of what it is like.

There are a number of, admittedly, hoary old questions which you can ask novelists which they seem to like answering. These include:

- To what extent do you plan your novels?
- Do you have a routine for writing?
- Do you hand-write or word-process?
- Are your characters based on people you know?
- Do they 'surprise' you by taking the plot off in unexpected directions?

I personally enjoy speaking to historical novelists because the research they do allows them to talk about the minutiae of the past – its smells, sights, sounds, buildings, customs and curiosities.

But however you approach interviewing writers always remember that the easiest way to antagonise them is to give the impression that you have no real interest in their work. This is easily done if you have not prepared properly.

Tony Wadsworth's interviewing tips

Sony Award winner Tony Wadsworth has worked in local radio for over 30 years. He has presented shows of all kinds and is presently Programme Editor at BBC Radio WM and Coventry and Worcester.

> It depends on the type of interview I'm doing, but as a rule if it's the 'softer' sort, I personally try to avoid talking too much to the interviewee beforehand . . . at least not about the subject we are going to be talking about. Experience has taught me that otherwise the guest can answer in one single response. I also avoid preparing questions in advance. I would rather

prepare a brief cue and then launch into the interview, listening carefully to what the guest has to say, posing relevant questions as I go. I remember very early on in my career, I had prepared a series of questions and got lengthy replies to the first two. The guest eventually completed his response and I asked him the next question on the list. Expecting a further lengthy reply, I mentally 'switched off' and began scanning my remaining questions to decide which ones to cut . . . when, to my surprise he suddenly ended his reply in one sentence. The result was that I was completely thrown and lost my train of thought. The ensuing silence was something I shall never forget. The moral? Listen to what the interviewee is saying and respond to what he or she says. I believe that the best interviews are conversational.

Tutorial

1. How would you define a good interview?
2. Who are the three best local radio interviewers in your area?

Seminar discussion

The best interviews appear to be a spontaneous chat between presenter and interviewee. Do you agree with this statement, if so why, if not why not? Write down five statements that support your position.

1. ______________________________
2. ______________________________
3. ______________________________
4. ______________________________
5. ______________________________

Practical assignment

1. Prepare an interview with a local politician about a contentious issue in your area.

2. Prepare an appropriate interview with a local beauty queen.

3. Prepare an interview on an incident in your local area from around 50 years ago. Go out and search for older people who remember the incident and carry out the interview.

3

Politicians, Pressure Groups and Powerful People

One-minute summary – Powerful people like local or national politicians need to use the media in order to get their message across to the public.

In this chapter you will learn:

- how to conduct a hard interview in a professional manner
- how to use the four things an interviewer has to do to create a good interview
- how to interview decision makers in your geographical area.

Who needs 'hard' questioning?

As the last chapter made clear, most of the time you will probably be conducting quite soft interviews on the programmes you present. Your interviewees will be only too pleased to answer your questions because they want to get across information to your audience.

However, you will also be interviewing people who are powerful because they are in a position to take decisions that affect our lives. Others are influential because they seek to persuade decision makers of the virtues of a policy or set of ideas. Others again are powerful because they manage industries or services and can do this efficiently, responsibly and cost-effectively, or otherwise.

I am thinking of such people as:

- politicians (local and national)
- industrialists and employers
- union leaders
- members of pressure groups and think tanks

- spokespersons for minority and other interests
- council officers.

I could go on, but doubtless you get the picture. These people will be arguing cases and defending positions and policies which need to be tested with other points of view and alternative ideas. In the case of politicians and other democratically elected people, they are in the position they are in because they have a mandate to be there. But it's part of the democratic process that their views are vigorously tested in public and shown up clearly for what they are.

Pressure groups, which advocate a change or changes in government or council policy, are also part of the legitimate democratic process. But it is important that we know where they are coming from, what exactly they are arguing and the implications of this.

It is also part of the media's function to hold such people as local NHS chiefs to account. Are they keeping to their charter commitments? Are they delivering an efficient and effective service?

In a sentence, all of these men and women need rigorous quizzing, or in the jargon, 'hard' questioning.

What is a 'hard' interview?

Holding people to account in the media by asking them perhaps unwelcome, certainly challenging questions is a relatively new idea.

There was a time, and it persisted into the late 1950s, when radio and television journalists simply lobbed easy and general questions at politicians and let them get on with it. The interviewees answered on their own terms, usually vaguely.

The man credited with changing that style of easy questioning and introducing what has become known as the 'inquisitorial style' is the late Sir Robin Day.

Day came to prominence as an interviewer on the BBC's *Panorama* programme in the early 1960s. He soon became known as a heavyweight performer and came under fire in some quarters for his 'insolent' tone towards politicians. Or, to put it another way, they began to be held to account because he wouldn't let them off the hook. By 1979 when he fronted the first edition of the television *Question Time* programme, he had developed a style of presentation characterised by one of his obituarists, Simon Heffer, in these terms: 'Day was able to use the programme to ride roughshod over the prevarications of politicians.' Heffer's summing up of Day is worth quoting: 'Robin Day's greatest achievement was to invent modern political interviewing as we know it. It was a craft he took exceptionally seriously, motivated by a desire to be a "seeker after truth", and to ask the questions that the public had a right to have answered. In doing so he made politicians more accountable to the public they claimed to serve.'

Those last two sentences sum up succinctly what 'hard' interviewing is all about and should act as a spur and an example to all who interview politicians and those who hold sway over public life. The hard interview is not merely an excuse for fireworks and controversy: it is an essential part of the democratic process in an open society.

Robin Day was the John the Baptist to that other political Grand Inquisitor, Jeremy Paxman. But before we go any further, I do not want suggest for a moment that anyone can simply *imitate* either of these and so become a successful interviewer.

As with everything you do, you have got to find your own way of doing things. Imitation might be the sincerest form of flattery, but if you simply imitate Paxman's aggressive style you will become a third rate Paxman when you should want to become a first rate you.

So, listen to your favourite interviewers. See how they go about their trade. Learn from them. But don't try to *be* them.

Preparation

All the obituaries of Sir Robin Day (he died in August 2000) commented on how well prepared he was for his set-piece interview. His probing questions grew out of a detailed knowledge of the person he was interviewing and the policies they were advocating.

His force of character, voice and personal idiosyncrasies made him an instantly recognisable figure. But his real authority came from a detailed knowledge of the political scene. For all his pugnacity he wanted, not to diminish politicians, but to get them to open up to the public and discuss their policies and ideas in a way which the public could understand.

This must be your aim. And unless you have the facts and knowledge at your fingertips your interviewee will be able to assert what he or she likes and get away with it. If a councillor says that in the last financial year £X thousand pounds was spent on libraries; if the Chief Constable tells you that clear-up rates have improved by Y% in the past 3 years; if the Chair of the local Health Trust says they are treating more prostate patients than ever before, you should have the ammunition to fire back if you think they are pulling a fast one, massaging the figures or not giving the entire statistical picture.

Media training

There is another good reason why research beforehand is vital. These days most professional front-men and women and virtually all MPs receive some sort of media training. Some people see this as a species of the black arts, but this is unfair. I've often found myself thinking, as a highly paid executive or spokesperson stumbles and rambles through an interview, that they could do with some proper media training to enable them to answer questions crisply and relevantly. But it's also true that media courses often train such people to avoid answering questions, bend interviews to their advantage and get across a pre-determined message rather than to engage meaningfully with the interviewer.

To the interviewer this can be a source of great frustration. Jeremy Paxman has written that 'listening to some senior figures speaking is like hearing one of those irritating BT call-waiting announcements ("the number you are calling knows you are waiting") and never getting put through.' And the broadcaster Robert Robinson has written of his experiences attempting to interview politicians during his stint presenting the BBC's *Today* programme:

> I thought interviewing politicians would be like interviewing anyone else, but it wasn't, since politicians are prevaricatory and evasive. Favourite openings by a Minister of the Crown when asked a plain question were 'What we've said – ' or perhaps 'We've made it quite plain – ' or possibly 'I've said very clearly – ' followed by rambling evasions.

Paxman and Robinson were writing of politicians in the highest flight of their profession and you will usually find local councillors, constituency MPs and other decision makers rather more amenable. But the fact remains that very frequently a great many people in public life have been taught to speak in sound-bites and schooled in holding a line by evading direct questions: they want to use the media to get a message across rather than engage in dialogue with the interviewer.

What can you do about this? The answer goes back to being well prepared. If you can be as well informed as your interviewee and make telling points the listener can judge for him or herself the validity of the interviewee's position and ideas.

Research

Your research will, of course take the form of reading the newspapers, drawing on your own accumulated knowledge, consulting news services and the internet. This is, arguably, the most useful of all research tools and you should be proficient at getting around useful sites and making use of what they can tell you.

Planning

There is such a thing as over preparing, however. The television presenter and former MP Brian Walden recalls preparing for set-piece interviews on the old *Weekend World* programme on ITV.

> There were four answers to any question really: yes; no; don't know; won't say. You know the charts of the kings of England, their descendents, the genealogical tables and all that – well I used to do that for the interviews. There would be the first question to which he or she would reply, yes/no/don't know/

> won't say, and there was a plan all the way through. If they said yes, well then I asked the next question, if they said no, then I would go to 39J. It was very carefully planned like that.

Well, that's one way to do it! In fact you won't have the time to plan an interview in anything like that detail. But even if you had, I wonder whether such an approach really yields dividends. Even a hard interview is a two way affair and the kind of machine-like precision of the Walden plan seems to me to militate against an interview which is entertaining and informative. Political junkies might love that sort of thing, the rest of us will probably find it a trifle arid.

Even so, Walden's general point, that how an interviewee answers one question may well determine the course of the rest of the interview is a good one. You must always listen to answers and be flexible enough to go off into unsuspected areas, always assuming that you think this will yield interesting results.

You must be prepared to be 'cheeky' and direct in your questioning. I once heard on a local radio station a Secretary of State for Health being interviewed. The presenter asked a perfectly reasonable question about waiting lists at the local hospital. The minister began to fire off volleys of statistics, some national, some local. These came so thick and fast that it was impossible to take them in. The presenter let this go. The minister moved on to listing the huge number of achievements in the health field her government had been responsible for. By this time I thought the presenter had dropped off and I was becoming more and more irritated. Why didn't he attempt to staunch this ludicrous and irrelevant flow of spurious eloquence? The minister ended up with a vision of the Golden Age yet to come to the NHS. By the time she finally stopped I was leaping up and down wishing I had small solid objects I could hurl at my radio. There was a pause. I found myself holding my breath. The presenter, in tones of sweet reasonableness, simply said: 'Thank you for that. Now you've said what *you* want to say please answer my question.'

I can't remember what the minister said after that, but in as much as ministers *can* sound chastened, she sounded it. Media training hadn't quite prepared her for that question.

But you see the problem. Like Robin Day, you should want to bring forth from the politicians and other powerful people a discussion of ideas and policy which will engage the electorate. You, like the listeners, want straight answers to fair questions. If the interviewee refuses to play that particular game you are left with a kind of point scoring. The cut and thrust of well ordered debate can simply become a sterile and rather meaningless exercise in which listeners will award points for 'performance' rather than anything more meaningful.

To avoid this, you've got to think carefully about your questions, and the tone you adopt. Let's now look at these two related areas.

Questions

Roger Mosey, of BBC news and a former editor of Radio 4's *Today* programme has written of tough interviewers like Jeremy Paxman and John Humphreys:

> They are the hired professionals. But that underestimates the high-wire act they perform in every interview. They need to know their own facts are correct and they have to be able to spot whoppers. They have to ask the questions the audience wants to ask, and also set the tone of a live broadcast.

This sums up very well the job that interviewers, from the superstars of *Newsnight* and *Today* down to the hacks who ply their trade in local radio stations, have to do.

Mosey mentions four things an interviewer has to do:

- know the subject
- spot 'whoppers'
- ask the right questions
- set the correct tone.

The first two are, of course, closely related. You can't spot when a politician or powerful person is massaging the truth or otherwise pulling a fast one unless you know the facts. Preparation is all-important, as I have emphasised above. The other two tasks an interviewer has to carry out are what interest us in this section.

By saying that an interviewer has 'to ask the questions the audience wants to ask' Mosey is implying that the presenter is acting on their behalf. And so, it follows that the interviewer shouldn't insinuate too much of his or her personality or ego into the proceedings. This is not, one must immediately say, to imply that the interviewer should be bland, anodyne or anonymous. Far from it. The best interviewers have a style and character of their own and these things lend their interviews a distinctiveness and flavour. But in the final analysis you are there as the servant of your listeners, not to harangue guests simply to draw attention to yourself.

This means that a *Today* interviewer will put different questions from those of a local radio presenter because their audiences are different and because the kind of interviewees will usually be different. The *Today* interviewer can be a bit more 'rarefied' than his or her counterpart at the local level. They can ask about the broad sweep of national policy as well as more particular questions.

Local issues

At the local level you'll most frequently be talking to men and women who either directly represent local people (local MPs and councillors, for example) or who make decisions directly affecting these people (Health Trust managers, local bus operators, for example). So you must frame questions which reflect how decisions will impact on your local audience.

Let us assume that the local council has decided to withdraw some services from housing estates and reallocate the money saved to education. In any interview with councillors about this it is important that you ask how this will affect the day to day life of residents of the estates in question. You must ask how the council can justify such a policy. How will the schools benefit? Will the policy result in money being effectively withdrawn from poor areas and spent disproportionately in high income areas? Will the decision result in higher crime rates because youth will have less to do? Will there be job losses?

The broader 'philosophical' questions about how you prioritise spending on education against spending on council run estates should of course be pursued vigorously. But your priority must be to confront your interviewee with the implications of their decisions for the people directly affected by those decisions.

If you *don't* ask those kinds of question you will not be giving a voice to your listeners and hence the localness of your station will be discounted.

One final point. For those in positions of power, the closed question, one which demands a one word answer, can be a very useful tool in your armoury. Jeremy Paxman won plaudits for an interview in which he asked the then Home Secretary, Michael Howard, the same closed question, 14 times. The fact that Mr Howard refused to answer a direct, simple question about a matter of fact was extremely revealing. An interview consisting entirely of closed questions would not work. But the occasional closed question on an important matter can be the lynch-pin of an interview.

Exercise

Choose a local news story about which there will be a number of views. It could be the decision to install speed bumps along a certain road, the withdrawal of one council service to fund another, or a change in the way bin collections are carried out. Now imagine that you have in the studio a person directly responsible for making such a decision. Draw up a list of questions you would put to him or her. Think especially about the kind of 'line' or arguments he or she is likely to push. How would you challenge such views?

Tone

I wrote earlier, rather flippantly, that Robin Day was John the Baptist paving the way for Jeremy Paxman. However, there are distinctions to be made between their two styles and attitudes.

Robin Day

Day was steeped in politics to the exclusion of virtually everything else. Remembering his friend, Sir Ludovic Kennedy has written of Day:

> In the 45 years I knew him, I never heard him express any interest in philosophy, religion, art, literature or even history, preferring to concentrate single-mindedly his skills and energies on what he knew best, the contemporary political scene.

Politics was his sole enthusiasm. He wanted to share that enthusiasm with his audience by encouraging us to take an informed interest in the doings of politicians, the decisions they took, the policies they espoused and put into operation. Thus a better informed and more interested electorate would be created.

Jeremy Paxman

Jeremy Paxman, it's not unfair to say, has an altogether more sceptical, some would say cynical, attitude towards politicians and the political process. He once said that when he interviewed a minister he always bore in mind the question: 'Why is this person sitting here lying to me?'

This kind of attitude, and the aggressive interviewing style which flows from it, can be effective. But it can also cause interviewees to become simply antagonistic and stonewall. Jeremy Paxman's style of interviewing is often entertaining, but it can produce more heat than light.

Balance

For what it's worth, my attitude towards politicians and other powerful people who come into my studio is one of scepticism rather than cynicism. Scepticism, because for perfectly understandable reasons they want to put the best possible construction or spin on their decisions and arguments and so it's my job to tease out whether what they say is valid, honest and sensible. But cynicism involves seeing people simply as self-serving, corrupt and dishonest.

Although some people in positions of power are undoubtedly like that, I am still optimistic enough about the public world, and the political world in particular, to believe that a good proportion of public figures want to do their best to improve things in their chosen field. They might be utterly mistaken in their decisions, but to treat every powerful figure as though they are cynically out for themselves will hardly result in enlightening interviews. Call me a wide-eyed innocent if you like! But inevitably the school of broadcasting will teach you lessons about public life and you must think about the implications of what you learn.

Nothing of what I have written absolves you from asking tough and well informed questions. Even if you accept that most people are in public life for reasonable motives, this doesn't mean to say that their decisions will always be right or that they're incapable of acting in an uninformed or inefficient manner. And this should be reflected in the tone you use.

The point should also be made that interviewing has become more difficult and aggressive since Sir Robin Day was in his prime because the nature of politics has changed. Jeremy Paxman himself has written:

> The reasons are multiple – globalisation, the EU, the role of the courts, privatisation, the centralisation of what remains of national power, the opaqueness of much parliamentary procedure, the decay of ideology and, yes, the influence of the mass media – to name but a few.

One might also add the iron grip the parties now exert on what can and cannot be said by MPs and ministers and the common occurrence of media training.

Local politicians

Even at the local level, huge changes have been made to the powers of local authorities. They have far less control over services and amenities than they did only a decade ago. The effect is that the local council often seems to be a kind of delivery system for the policies of the national government. Certainly all councils are now far more dependent on funding from Westminster than once they were.

The effect is to create an illusion of local democracy whilst increasingly the real decisions are made directly or indirectly at Westminster. This means the local councillors to whom you speak will often point the finger of blame at Westminster when cuts in local services are made and yet will still make great claims for what their party can do come election time.

All of this often makes interviewing local politicians a very frustrating business. But if local democracy means anything, it means our local representatives taking responsibility for their decisions, and it's part of your job to enforce that message in the question you put and the tone you adopt.

Part of that tone is bound up with knowing when to interrupt, and this is a skill which you will need to develop. Again there are no rules here. This is something which comes from experience and observation.

If you interrupt too much you risk antagonising your audience who may genuinely want the interviewee to finish a sentence or a point without the presenter butting in. On the other hand, if you simply let an interviewee set their own agenda, then you won't have done your job properly.

Roger Mosey has some very pertinent things to say about this:

> Audiences value Paxman and Humphreys because they won't let politicians get away with waffle and evasion. It's equally dangerous to suggest that interviewers should eschew interruption. Chopping off guests a few seconds after they've opened their mouths isn't a good idea. But neither is it acceptable for a politician to filibuster without being brought back to the point.

Often an interview can fail because an interviewer misjudges an intervention. Even highly experienced interviewers can make mistakes – but after a time you should develop a feel for when an intervention is appropriate and necessary.

Meanwhile, listen carefully to how interviewers keep interviews on the tracks.

Exercise

Record a radio or TV interview in which a politician or other public figure is being interviewed by a 'heavyweight'. Listen to it a number of times noting the specific questions and occasions on which the interviewer interrupts the guest. Write a brief note on each of these interruption saying why you think the interviewer made that interruption, whether it was justified and what effect it had.

This is bound to be a very subjective analysis. But the purpose is to get you to think hard about interruptions and how successful they can be in getting a guest to answer relevantly the questions put.

Alternative styles

There are, of course, other ways of questioning the powerful apart from the Paxman/Humphreys style. David Frost at his best, for example, employs a style which is relaxed, cheeky and occasionally hard when the interviewee least expects it. It's a style which can strike one as bland. But Frost is a highly experienced interviewer, is formidably prepared and gets a lot out of his guests by asking 'obvious' questions and ever so politely not letting them off the hook.

And the veteran Irish radio interviewer and television chat-show host (now retired) Gay Byrne managed to get some extraordinary interviews out of politicians just by being so relaxed that their defences slipped.

This style and tone of interviewing is, if anything more difficult that the aggressive style pioneered by Day. You can only really do it if you have a genuinely charismatic broadcasting presence and a willingness to take considerable risks. If it fails, this kind of apparently 'soft' interviewing can seem bland and lazy. But it can yield dividends: the powerful have come to expect aggressive questions and when they get something else the effect can be pleasingly disconcerting. Kenneth Clarke in Paul Donovan's history of the *Today* programme is quoted as saying: 'You can get into more trouble with a friendly interviewer than with a combative one.'

Breaking the rules

As I have remarked, the golden rule is that there is no golden rule. Even as you formulate the kind of questions you think your audience will want to hear, you must be prepared to junk those questions if you realise that an interview would be more entertaining and informative if it went off in another direction.

For example, not long ago I spoke to an American advice columnist called Don Savage. He had written a book called *The Kid.* This is an entertaining account of what happened when Savage and his boyfriend decided to adopt a baby. He writes in detail about the process, their relationship with the baby's mother, the reaction of family and friends, and generally explores the feelings and issues involved in the decision.

As I skimmed the book, I began to jot down ideas for questions. Don Savage is not a member of the powerful elite which need tough questioning. But his book is contentious and I was under no illusion about what listeners would think about Don Savage's ideas. I wanted to let him give an idea of the problems he had encountered in the adoption process and why he and his partner wanted to do it. But I also wanted to challenge him, as I thought our listeners would, on whether it's a good idea to bring up a boy with no female example in the house, whether adoption is a right or a privilege, whether the kind of open adoption which is available in the States but not over here really works... in other words I wanted to put him on the spot and test the certainties of his book.

When he came on the line he turned out to be a witty, charming, eloquent talker whose account of the adoption process was vivid, entertaining and moving. I realised after a few minutes that I just wanted to hear what he had to say about his experiences, so I disregarded most of my questions and nudged him through his story ending up with a couple of harder questions.

Was I right to take this decision? Perhaps not. Perhaps I was a victim of his charm and eloquence. But in the event we received one, admittedly irate, complaint about the immorality of allowing such a piece to go on at all, and one saying it was a gripping piece of radio.

My own feelings about gay adoption were, of course, neither here nor there. What mattered ultimately was that people heard someone's story and experiences and so could, if they wanted to make up their own minds on the subject.

Sometimes listeners want the interviewer simply to tease out a story with the minimum of interventions. Knowing when to shut up and let the guest get on with it is a valuable skill. And it really only comes with experience.

Pressure groups

Pressure groups are now part of the political process. Organisations like the Child Poverty Action Group, Age Concern, Charter 88, the Campaign for the Protection of Rural England, Transport 2000 and all the rest, commission research, lobby MPs and generally try to get their message across in a way which will influence public policy.

There is, of course, nothing wrong with this at all. However, pressure groups, because they *are* a part of the political process, need rigorous interviewing.

Very frequently, the policies of such groups would require an increase in public expenditure if they were to be adopted by government. For example, Age Concern want an increase in the retirement pension and often produce policy statements and research to back this up. Similarly, the Child Poverty Action Group frequently issue demands for an increase in benefits for the worse off.

It is perfectly legitimate to make such demands. But it is equally legitimate to ask representatives of such groups where the extra money required should come from. Single issue pressure groups need to be confronted with the wider implications of their stated demands.

I also find myself asking questions about whether they are being politically realistic in their aims – whether, indeed their demands can ever be met. You occasionally come across pressure groups who resemble Reg's revolutionary party in *Monty Python's Life of Brian* ('We're giving Pilate two days to dismantle the entire apparatus of the Roman Imperialist State.') I once found myself talking to someone who represented a group which simply wanted to do away with cars as quickly as possible. It's also important to ask about the level of support for the group.

You will also have to talk to the *ad hoc* groups which spring up in response to a local situation. These might be demanding a by-pass, rejecting speed bumps along a certain road, objecting to a library or school closure or protesting at the reduction in services provided by a neighbourhood centre.

Again, in these cases it is important to challege them about whether they really have got the support they always say they have and to confront them with the implications of their demands. One has to be quite careful, but often you can give tacit support to some of these groups. For example, if the local authority is refusing to provide a lollipop lady on a busy road outside a school, you have got to be sympathetic to the concerned parents.

Nevertheless, it is important that you don't unthinkingly side with any pressure group which happens along. To the best of your ability, check it out, make sure it is properly constituted, that it does genuinely reflect substantial local feeling and is not just an unrepresentative group of the disaffected few. Only then can you take it seriously or otherwise.

Impartiality

It might seem odd to follow that comment with an assertion of your necessary impartiality.

The BBC's Producer Guidelines state:

> Due impartiality lies at the heart of the BBC. It is a core value and no area of programming is exempt from it.

As a presenter, this particularly refers to political impartiality. Whatever station you work for, BBC or independent, party political impartiality is expected by listeners.

I once asked the former political editor of the BBC, John Cole, what this meant in his case. He had been a print journalist before joining the Corporation and so was used to a situation in which he was able to vent his own feelings and allegiances rather more freely than in the organisation he subsequently joined.

> It was very simple. I made a self-denying ordinance: I wouldn't let my own political views in any way colour what I

> was reporting for the BBC. Any professional should be able to do this.

John Cole's 'self-denying ordinance' is one we all have to take. In fact, in all the years I've worked in broadcasting and mixed on a daily basis with broadcast journalists and presenters, I can only remember a tiny handful of people who had strong political allegiances and were willing to share them in private conversation. For most broadcasters, the political process and the stories it throws up are what matter. Whether you happen to agree or disagree with the policies or doings of a particular party is neither here nor there.

One journalist I knew made no secret of the fact that she supported the Conservative Party, though she was strictly impartial in her reporting. Nevertheless, I remember her news editor sending her out to interview a rising Conservative minister who was visiting the area with words, the gist of which were: 'And if you don't give him a proper grilling, there'll be hell to pay!'

She came back with a tape which satisfied her editor. She would have done so anyway, but her boss was making sure she was well aware of the score when it came to bias.

However, when you are on the air day in day out discussing current issues it is sometimes difficult not to allow your political views to emerge over time. This means that you must be aware of the number of sides to any question or policy. Playing devil's advocate should be second nature to you.

Sir Robin Day stood as a parliamentary candidate for the Liberal Party before he became a television journalist. But in all his years as an interviewer he showed no bias in that direction. And I defy anyone who can deduce from the questions they put, the political allegiances, if any, of Jeremy Paxman, John Humphreys, Kirsty Wark or any of the heavyweights who grace the airwaves today.

Humphreys, tackled on this, said:

> I do not express political opinions and nobody would be able to judge...what my political views are. The BBC does not require its presenters not to have any views on anything, it

requires its presenters not to make their political views explicit, for very obvious reasons.

Even if you play precisely by the rule-book, you will still receive complaints of bias. These need to be answered fairly and you and your producer, who should be monitoring you for on-air bias all the time, will need constantly to review your own performance in the light of complaints.

I reckon I get as many complaints saying I veer to the left as saying I veer to the right. Which, I hope, indicates the professional neutrality we should all aim for.

Tutorial

1. What are soft and hard interviews?
2. What are the three functions of a cue?
3. What is a pressure group?

Seminar discussions

As a broadcaster you have to talk to all areas of the political spectrum. To what extent should a broadcaster be expected to give airtime to those who hold unfavourable political views, like terrorists or racist organisations?

Practical assignments

1. Visit your Town Hall and find out the names of your local councillors/representatives and the wards/locations they represent.

2. What are the future developments that may cause a row, in your area? For example a new shopping centre, new road, pedestrianisation.

4

The Phone-In

One-minute summary – The phone-in, at least in Britain, was the invention of local radio. A few months after BBC Radio Leicester, the first local radio station in this country, came on the air in 1967, the manager had the bright idea of allowing listeners to speak directly to the station's gardening expert. The experiment was a success and thus the phone-in was born. Since then it has become a feature of all speech based stations. (For more on this, see Chapter 7.)

In this chapter, you will learn:

- why the phone-in is such a vital part of your future programme
- how phone-ins are produced and your role as a presenter
- how to present the one to one phone-in
- how to present the single subject phone-in
- how Baroness Thatcher was challenged over the sinking of a ship in the Falklands War.

The importance of the phone-in

Why are phone-ins so important? One answer is given in the BBC's Producers' Guidelines: 'They allow the public direct access to air their own views and to question politicians and other public figures'.

Access is the key word here. The phone-in gives access to decision makers and hence an important democratic principle is furthered and upheld. But because that access is facilitated by the radio station, the phone-in promotes a sense of 'ownership' amongst listeners. One of the reasons why people have a different attitude to their local radio station (and it *is*, in an important sense, *their* radio station) is that they can use it to talk to each other and to the people who make decisions which affect their lives.

A local radio station is in one sense like a garden wall across which neighbours gossip, exchange news and views and argue. In another sense it is like a public meeting at which individuals can directly address public figures with thousands of other people listening.

The phone-in, then, is a significant community resource and an important means by which listeners connect with and relate to the station. At its best, the general phone-in, where listeners can simply talk about what is on their minds, is the community talking to itself.

There is another way in which phone-ins are valuable to a station: they generate more broadcast material. A listener complaining bitterly about the inefficiency shown by the local authority or the water company is a cue for the producer to pursue the organisations on the listener's behalf. How the bodies complained of respond on air when they are tackled by the presenter and/or the original complainer should make interesting listening.

Moreover, news material is often generated by phone-ins. If there is a genuine feeling that the station has an 'open door' policy all sorts of stories will emerge on air which broadcast journalists can and should follow up.

At this point it should be said that for all their popularity, phone-ins are far from easy to present. Indeed, they are, arguably, the most difficult element in a station's output to bring off successfully.

The phone-in, by its very nature, is spontaneous and unpredictable. The presenter has got to be quick-witted, well briefed, always on top of the situation and, given the potential for the law to be broken and offence to be given, they have got to be able to extricate the programme from difficult situations with speed and in a natural-sounding manner. A phone-in presenter *must* have a good working knowledge of the law of defamation and contempt. (These matters are dealt with in the next chapter.)

But the success or otherwise of a phone-in isn't solely down to the presenter. It is a team effort and it is to this that we now return.

The production of phone-ins

If you are very lucky you will have a three person team for a phone-in sequence: the presenter, the producer and a phone answerer. Given the economics of most stations, the last two functions are usually combined.

The presenter's relationship with the producer is a key element in the success of a phone-in. The presenter has got to be confident of the decisions the producer makes, but equally the producer has got to be confident of the abilities of the presenter. A presenter who is only able to cope with bland and uncontentious calls will hardly set the airwaves alight.

Even the most confident and experienced of presenters must be able to take on-air production in the form of advice on when to move on, when to speed up or rein back, possible responses to callers, and so on. Not that a presenter wants a producer chattering away in the headphones the whole time! On-air-over-production is worse than no production at all. The occasional nudge from the producer is important. This can stop the sequence from sounding self-indulgent or lazy and bring a fresh perspective to bear on the debates in hand.

Above all, the producer and presenter must work in harmony to set the *pace* of the sequence. As far as possible, there must always be a call standing by that the presenter can go to whenever the on-air call has come to a natural conclusion. Judging when that moment has come is something that develops with experience. But even an experienced presenter can get bogged down in a call and the producer need to keep tabs on the output and tell the presenter when to move on.

Given all this, some kind of debriefing after the programme is always helpful. Producers and presenters should be able to exchange professional views frankly. The producer must be able to tell the presenter how they performed. Equally, a presenter should be able to question the producer's decisions about the ordering of calls, and so on. A natter about how the programme went and how it might have been improved will always yield dividends. No one is too old to learn.

Kinds of phone-in

There are two kinds of phone-in. One consists of a presenter fielding calls from listeners. The other involves a guest or guests in the studio to whom the listeners direct questions and comments.

As we shall see, within these two categories there are distinctions and sub-divisions. But let us start with the simplest kind of phone-in, the one you will most commonly hear on local radio stations.

The 'one to one' phone-in

Within this category there are two sub-divisions:

- The general phone-in.
- The single subject phone-in.

The former involves opening the lines for any subject the callers want to discuss. In the latter, the presenter firmly 'sets the agenda' and invites calls on a specific subject, usually, of course, one of the topical issues, local or national, of the day. Both require preparation, but let us take the former first.

The general phone-in

It should go without saying that before presenting a general phone-in you should have good sense of what is in the news that day. So you must scan the newspapers, local and national, especially the ones your listeners are likely to be reading. Monitor your station's news bulletins for talking points. Make sure you know what programmes have been on the television the previous night, especially if they have been flagged as controversial. The various news sites of the internet should also be consulted if you have time.

You will be looking for talking points of various kinds.

Firstly, there are the issues of the day which promote debate either because they arouse strong emotions or because there are several views on the subject. The classic topics here are corporal punishment, capital punishment, the EU, law and order. But beware, a simple diet of this sort of thing can be very tiresome. The object must be to take the news of the day and *make* it debatable. This can be done in various ways.

Suppose the local council has decided to install speed bumps along a certain road. A number of views might be forthcoming on this and they may be prompted by asking such questions as this:

- Do you think speed bumps really work?
- If you live along the road in question, is it really that dangerous for pedestrians?
- If so, will the proposal make the situation better?

In addition, phone the local bus company to get their response to the decision. Ask questions such as:

- Will their vehicles be affected?
- Will the bumps disrupt the time-table?
- Will it make for an uncomfortable ride?

Try to 'seed' your phone-in with calls from people who can bring a fresh perspective on the topics of the day.

Don't be afraid to be opinionated. Most people don't like speed bumps so I tend to argue strongly for them on the grounds that the official figures show that they do save lives, especially those of children. What is a bit of inconvenience compared with a human life?

So ask questions but also give listeners something to argue with.

You should also localise national news. If the government announces an increase in funding for the police or NHS ask your listeners how that money should be spent locally. Do you want another police helicopter or more bobbies on the beat? If you have been in the local hospital recently, how would you like to see the money spent? Do you get a good service from your GP? If not, how could the money be spent to help him or her?

Without trivialising the news, try to bring issues down to the level to which your listeners can respond.

Lighter topics

Secondly, there are lighter topics which will provoke uncontentious but entertaining calls. Earlier in the week in which I write this, one newspaper carried news of an invention designed to insert duvets into duvet covers with the minimum of fuss. In fact, this remarkable technological step forward sounds very complicated and involves the manipulation of two hinged aluminium poles. I mentioned the contraption and asked whether anyone had easier ways of doing this household chore. This provoked a good number of calls which had the virtue of passing on useful tips and leavening an otherwise rather stodgy sequence. But it also developed into a discussion of whether duvets are better than sheets and blankets, when duvets began to be the bed covering of choice . . . and before the end of the sequence we were getting calls about how labour saving devices had transformed housework.

Put baldly like this, the calls might sound trivial. But in fact they were expressions of lived social history, interesting in themselves and, as I've remarked, an important element in the mix of the sequence.

Thirdly, there are topics which evoke nostalgia. Clearly, this is an area of discussion unsuitable for some stations and sequences. But if your listenership has a good proportion of older people, then 'heritage radio' as it has come to be called, will be an important part of your phone-in.

Historical anniversaries are obviously a good prompt for calls of this kind. When the 60th anniversary of the Battle of Britain was being commemorated over the summer and autumn of 2000 memories of the sights and sounds and events of 1940 were not difficult to prompt. There were a number of television documentaries about the subject and their coverage and interpretation of events and their historical significance provided talking points.

Local and national news generally provide one or two topics of this kind every day. The demolition of an old factory, the closure of a local shop, a change in the licensing laws, harvest and seed-time, changes to the school curriculum, the death of a sporting celebrity . . . all will furnish occasions to draw out your listeners' memories.

Your aim should be to provide a good mix of topics on your phone-in. Of course, on some days one overwhelmingly important subject will dominate proceedings. But on most days your phone-in will probably be varied in terms of subject matter and tone, from the rancorous and opinionated to the light and nostalgic.

Exercise

Imagine you are presenting a phone-in sequence today. Make a list of the topics you would 'throw out' at the beginning of the programme. Aim for about eight or ten subjects of different kinds. The mix should vary from the 'hard' topics making the news to nostalgic and light ones. Work out how you might announce these topics. What questions would you ask? What opinions might you express to give listeners something to argue with?

Your performance

How you respond to your callers sets the tone for your phone-in. If you want to be a 'shock-jock' and simply bait your listeners and be provocative for the sake of it, well you don't need any advice from me.

But even within 'main-stream', responsible programmes you can hear a range of approaches and tones being taken by presenters.

Broadly speaking, presenters on the big metropolitan stations sound rather more aggressive and outspoken than their counterparts on smaller stations and those serving more rural areas. Each station has an overall sound or tone and you will have to adjust your performance to what is required.

However, no station wants to sound simply bland and unmemorable. You can be challenging and opinionated without being rude; you can be provocative without alienating listeners who prefer cosiness to fireworks. But it's a difficult tight-rope to walk. No matter how experienced you become you and your producer should be constantly monitoring your performance.

A note on late evening programmes is appropriate at this point.

Traditionally, such programmes have taken on 'broader' and more controversial themes than their day-time equivalents. Again, you will have to tailor your performance to the needs of your station. But given the contentious material with which you will be dealing, your sense of when someone is over-stepping the mark, both legally and in terms of taste, will have to be highly honed. Even more than on a day-time sequence your relationship with the producer must be one of the utmost trust.

Presenting a late evening sequence is often exciting and rewarding – but it is fraught with dangers and needs great experience and sensitivity.

Your over-riding concern should be to produce a sequence which is entertaining. If it is as dull as ditch water no one will want to know. And, depending on your audience, they will be entertained by a mixture of controversy, humour, information, nostalgia . . . and of course, good talk!

Single subject phone-ins

Much of what I have written above applies to the single subject phone-in. However, it must be said that this sort of phone-in can be difficult to bring off for at least two reasons.

Firstly, the topic has got to be of a kind which will sustain a single sequence. It is not easy to come up with such subjects on a daily basis. Clearly, you will have to be very inventive in making a subject interesting or contentious enough to get listeners calling in large enough numbers and with enough points of view to keep the sequence moving. It goes without saying that the presenter has got to know the topic in question inside out.

Secondly, there is always the danger of lack of variety.

In a general phone-in, when you switch topics you will often change your tone. This helps to keep boredom at bay and combats blandness. So built into the general phone-in is a kind of resistance to sameness.

One of the secrets of keeping a single topic phone-in fresh is to set up calls from interested parties beforehand. These can be interspersed throughout the sequence, ensuring that a number of different slants on the topic are heard.

The presenter should not be afraid of taking up a number of positions on an issue. Consistency isn't a virtue if it doesn't provoke good calls.

Phone-ins with guests

Broadly speaking, phone-ins involving guests are of three kinds:

- Those involving politicians and other public figures.
- Those involving representatives of service industries.
- Those involving 'experts'.

A general point can be made about all three. The important people in this context are the callers and the guests. The phone-in here is providing direct access to people whom the listeners, for various reasons, wish to talk to. Unlike in a straight interview, you are not the listeners' representative. It is your job to facilitate that access by helping out the caller if they become tongue-tied or find it difficult to get to the point, preventing the guest from straying off the point and generally keeping the sequence moving along. You are a *presence* in such phone-ins, but not the *focus*.

Politicians and public figures
As I have remarked earlier, politicians these days are trained in how to cope with media interviews and are well versed in the tactics of obfuscation and avoidance. But when an ordinary member of the public tackles them in a direct and artless way the results can be interesting

Case study

The set-to between a geography teacher, Mrs Diana Gould from Chichester, and the Prime Minister, Margaret Thatcher, during the Falklands War has gone down in media history. The subject was the controversial sinking of the Argentinian warship the *Belgrano*, with the loss of many lives.

> MARGARET THATCHER: *My duty was to look after our troops, our ships, our navy, and my goodness me I lived with many, many anxious days and nights.*
>
> DIANA GOULD: *Mrs Thatcher, you started your answer by saying the 'Belgrano' was not sailing away from the Falklands. It was on a bearing of 280 and it was already west of the Falklands, so I'm sorry, but I cannot see how you can say it was not sailing away from the Falklands.*

MT: *When it was sunk it was a danger to our ships...*

DG: *No, but you have just said at the beginning of your answer that it was not sailing away from the Falklands, and I am asking you to correct that statement.*

MT: *Yes, but in an area outside the exclusion zone, which I think is what you are saying is sailing away.*

DG: *No, I'm not. I am asking which way it was facing at the time. I am saying that it was on a bearing of 280, which is a bearing of just north of west. It was already west of the Falklands and therefore nobody with any imagination can put it sailing any other than away from the Falklands.*

MT: *Mrs... I'm sorry, I've forgotten your name.*

DG: *Mrs. Gould...*

It is, admittedly, rare to come across a listener as well prepared and tenacious as Diana Gould. But this exchange, in the words of the broadcaster Ian Hargreaves, illustrates the fact that 'it is harder for a politician to slap down an ordinary voter than a celebrity broadcaster'.

On a local radio phone-in you are very unlikely to hear an exchange like the one above, but it can happen. You are more likely to hear a local council leader being tackled by council-tax payers who are complaining about the inefficiency of services and amenities provided by the authority. Callers can speak directly from the heart of their own experience and it is difficult for councillors to evade such complaints. If they do it's the presenter's job to help the caller if such help is needed. 'You have broken the pledge of your latest charter, what are you going to do now to remedy the situation?' I hear myself saying words like this often when conducting such phone-ins. The listeners can do the talking, it's your job to be their champion *when and if they need it*, by insisting that the guest does something to address the complaint.

Guests from service industries/organisations

Many stations run phone-ins with representatives from the Inland Revenue, the Benefits Agency, bus operators, the Royal Mail and so on. These have the virtue of allowing people who have dealings with such organisations and services to speak directly to people who can remedy a situation if it needs remedying. Again, the presenter must act as a champion for callers if that role is called for.

But there is a draw back. Mrs X's problem in getting the benefit which is due to her is, of course, of burning interest to Mrs X, but will be of interest to no one else unless they are in exactly Mrs X's position. Similarly with complaints about the 54 bus or question 17b on the Income Tax form.

There is not much that can be done about this if the station feels that such phone-ins are worth doing. But for what it's worth, I think it's much better to invite such guests in and allow them five minutes on the air to establish their presence and then invite calls off-air. At the end of the session (perhaps 45 minutes) they can come on-air again to say what kind of calls they've had and what others suffering from similar problems can do.

Even this is unsatisfactory because the guests are not being heard to be held to account in public. But long public service phone-ins, for reasons mentioned above, can be terribly boring.

If you do have to present such a phone-in sequence, the secret is to keep the pace up. The producer should select calls which raise significant general as well as specific points. And the organisations concerned should be encouraged to supply guests who are properly trained and who can deal with the public sympathetically and in an interesting fashion. This is by no means always the case!

Phone-ins with experts

Listening to someone who has a genuine enthusiasm for a subject and is able to communicate that enthusiasm spontaneously is one of the pleasures of broadcasting. Such people are gems and you should make good use of them.

Very often their use is prompted by an off-air question. Recently we had a call on my programme about an old bottle which a listener had dug up in his garden. Did the name inscribed on it mean anything to anyone? Was it collectable?

This prompted a number of other calls and after a bit of research we discovered a local bottle collector with a wealth of information at his finger-tips. My producer reckoned we should field him for a phone-in session on the subject. I was dubious. How many people would phone us on that, on the face of it, rather obscure subject?

I was wrong, of course. Our guest was a natural and prompted dozens of calls, not just about specific bottles but about the flavours of fizzy drink you could get in the old days, working in bottling plants, recycling glass, etc, etc.

Expert guests, whether their subject is wild-life, cigarette cards, soap operas, local history, medical matters, hand writing or whatever, need to be able to speak in ways the audience can understand. If they can do this you, the presenter, will have to do very little except sit back, introduce callers and listen to enthusiastic words of wisdom as the sequence unfolds. This is a joy!

Final thoughts

When I started as a full-time radio presenter I asked a man of huge radio experience what the secret of presenting a good phone-in was. How did he *know* what topics would get the phones alight.

He grinned and said: 'It beats me. Always remember that you know nothing!'

I've often thought of those words in ensuing years. I've lost count of the number of times I've gone into the studio at the start of a phone-in convinced that listeners would call in their droves because there were at least half a dozen gold-plated, copper-bottomed stories in the news about which everyone would want to have a say...only to find that the great British public had something better to do and silence reigned, save for my increasingly desperate attempt to get somebody, *anybody*, to call us.

Conversely, on days which from the news point of view are alarmingly quiet, people have phoned in with fascinating comments, stories and observations and the result has been a great programme.

The ways of the world are a mystery, and the good presenter approaches the task of making a phone-in work with some humility!

Ed Doolan's phone-in thoughts

Ed Doolan MBE has worked for 30 years as a radio broadcaster. He's won many industry awards including a Sony. He's worked at Birmingham's BBC Radio WM since 1982 where his Sunday to Friday phone-in programme has won him the title the 'consumer's champion'. Of the phone-in he says this:

> Strange animal this. Anyone can do it – badly.
>
> Why do we listen to a phone-in? To learn? To participate? To scoff? To hear what the NEXT caller has to say?
>
> It's dangerous when done properly. It's unpredictable. It's exhausting.
>
> Why do we phone a phone-in? Loneliness? Ego? To genuinely offer knowledge, information or a yet not stated view?
>
> I have a theory that however much you may be above phoning a radio station, the moment will one day come when you find that you are the only person listening with the definitive answer to a question being posed. Even Superman could not keep off the line.
>
> Prime Minister Margaret Thatcher called Radio 4, Sir Paul McCartney called in to 2SM Sydney and even a Home Secretary once phoned CWR, the popular Midlands Radio station.
>
> The draw is irresistible.

Tutorial

1. Why are phone-ins important?

2. What single subject topics would work well on your programme?

3. What phone-ins are taking place on radio today, in your area?

Seminar discussion

The phone-in provides access for the general public, to matters of importance. It could be argued therefore that the phone-in is good for democracy. Why is it good for democracy?

Practical assignment

1. Listen in to a phone-in on a BBC or public service radio station in your area. Make a point of calling the station and getting a comment on air.

2. Try calling a phone-in on a national radio station and getting your point on air. This will help you to understand what callers experience when they call your programme.

5

Broadcasting and the Law

One-minute summary – Speech based radio is live, unscripted and spontaneous. So the potential for a station to break the law relating to defamation (which deals with a slur on reputation) and contempt (which deals with active court cases) is great. This chapter refers to the state of the law in the United Kingdom, in particular in England, Wales and Northern Ireland. If you live outside this area, you will need to determine the law requirements in your area.

In this chapter you will learn about:

- defamation and how to avoid falling foul of the law
- contempt and how to stay out of trouble
- the three defences to libel.

Knowledge of the law

The phone-in is the most difficult area in this respect. Most people who phone a station will have only the haziest notion of the law in these areas and many will think there is nothing wrong in repeating on air gossip they heard in the pub the previous evening. I am still taken aback when I hear that listeners have wanted to raise the issue of a local personality's sexual proclivities, the 'fact' that a local councillor is well known to be corrupt or that a person appearing in court is, of course, guilty of the crime of which he or she is accused.

It's the job of the producer to filter out such dangerous callers and ensure that they don't get the opportunity to utter such sentiments on air. Were they to do so the station could well be sued for substantial sums. But of course it's impossible to know exactly what a caller (or interviewee, for that matter) will say once they are on air and so the potential for breaking the law will always be there. As a presenter you must have a good working knowledge of the law so that you yourself don't breach it and so that you can interrupt or cut someone off when they begin to stray towards dangerous territory.

What follows is a very general guide to the law of defamation and contempt as they relate to the speech radio presenter. **This is, to emphasise the point, only a guide and does not replace specialised advice.** No summary can cover all the legal issues in this area and you should familiarise with one or other of the standard books on the subject. These are McNae's *Essential Law for Journalists*, *Media Law for Journalists* by Robertson and Nicol, or *Scots Law for Journalists* by McKain, Bonnington and Watt. (There are differences between the legal systems of England and Scotland and you may need to know these.) If your station does not have a copy of one or other of these volumes, make sure it purchases one!

If you have taken a post-graduate journalism course you will be taught the law in this field. However, it is always a good thing to refresh your knowledge of the subject periodically. The law is complicated and its nuances can easily be forgotten.

Defamation

If a station broadcasts anything which injures the reputation of an individual, a group or an organisation it may be libelling them. It is important to note that it is the broadcasting organisation which is liable, no matter who actually speaks the words. This is because that organisation is deemed to be the 'publisher' of those words. So if a caller to a BBC phone-in utters a libel, it's the BBC which will get sued if the person defamed decides to go to court.

What, then, constitutes libel? The problem is that there is no actual definition, though over the years various judges have laid down guide-lines. Judges usually tell juries that a statement about a person is defamatory if it does one or other of the following:

- Exposes him/her to hatred, ridicule or contempt.
- Causes him/her to be shunned or avoided.

- Reduces him/her in the estimation of right-thinking members of society generally.
- Disparages him/her in their business, office, trade or profession.

Even these guide-lines are vague (what is 'right thinking', for example?), but most libellous allegations attack someone's reputation either personally or professionally. You should bear in mind this rule of thumb: if you were that person would you like this allegation made about yourself. So, if you hear a caller or guest stating something which falls into this category always err on the side of caution and interrupt or cut them off. In fact, if you are in any way concerned that what someone is saying may fall foul of the law *always err on the side of caution.*

Having said that, there are a number of defences to libel. These are:

- justification
- privilege
- fair comment.

Justification

The defence of justification means roughly this. If the broadcast story or allegation is true and you have sufficient evidence to stand up in a court of law and prove your case, then you have no problem. However, there is often a difficulty in securing that evidence. Clearly a guest or caller who, for example, simply alleges that person X is a paedophile must be cut off as soon as possible. In all probability it will be very difficult to obtain evidence for such an allegation, and even if you did, securing that evidence in court will probably be very difficult. This defence depends utterly on your being able to provide a watertight case.

Privilege

This is a complicated area. But in essence, statements made during broadcasts of fair and accurate reports of judicial proceedings, public meetings and parliamentary proceedings will have privilege in a libel case. In other words, you are generally safe to report words said in these three contexts.

However, there are problems for presenters even here. A guest or caller may well have read a court report in a newspaper and repeat a garbled and defamatory version of it on-air. In which case a libelled person may well have reason to sue.

Fair comment

One authority on the law of journalism writes: 'Fair comment is one of the most difficult defences to explain because it is almost indefinable!' This is, indeed a difficult area. But fair comment must:

- Be based on fact or truth.
- Be an opinion honestly held.
- Be on a matter of public interest.
- Be without malice.

Of these, the third point is the most vague because it is the most far reaching. It can cover public affairs and the people involved in them, the arts, sport, TV, entertainment and consumer affairs. But what constitutes 'public interest'?

As a guide, fair comment should be based on an individual's public standing, not his or her personal life. The whole question of what is of public interest has been raised frequently in recent years: a person's sexuality or extra-marital sexual activities are probably of little public interest unless, of course, that person is a public servant and happens to be acting hypocritically and deceiving the people he or she is supposed to be representing.

But, to repeat, this is a very grey area. A caller or interviewer may well think that what he or she is saying is fair comment, but a court may well take a very different view. Be careful!

Is the other party likely to sue?

This is a question which comes to the forefront during consumer phone-ins (but not exclusively in that context). In these, it is not uncommon to hear callers complain about companies, retailers, manufacturers and so on, in terms which could well be defamatory. Although producers often tell callers to make *general* points and mention no names this advice is often ignored.

Here are a few comments I've recently heard on the station on which I work and on others. (The names, have of course, been changed to head off legal action!)

> I've had no end of trouble with Bloggs' on the High Street. They sold me a washing machine two months ago and it's been nothing but trouble. I've had the repairers in three times and it still rattles. It's a dodgy outfit and I shan't be going back.

> I bought a reconditioned car at Blue's Garage. It went alright for about six weeks. Then it broke down and my son-in-law, who knows about cars reckons it'll cost me almost as much as I paid for it to get it repaired. They don't want to know about this and I think they ought to be closed down if they go on...

> I took my holiday film to Yellow's and when I got it back it was the wrong film...the wrong photos. I took them back but they weren't interested. They refunded my money but they couldn't be bothered to try to find my film.

You can hear comments like this on phone-ins with Trading Standards officers on local radio stations up and down the land. Technically, it's quite possible that all of them constitute a libel. However, so long as the companies in question are given the right of reply if they request it, or if the programme offers them this right by asking them for a response to the allegations you should be in the clear.

But, and it's a big but, you must be aware that some companies are extremely litigious and will send out a letter threatening to sue at the drop of a hat. So again, you must be very careful what you permit callers to say. For example, the description of Bloggs' as a 'dodgy outfit' could be construed as very damaging, especially if it is a local company. And bear in mind that large companies employ radio monitors to listen to stations across the country so they can be aware of comments and allegations broadcast about them. It is not a reasonable argument to say that you will broadcast what you like on the grounds that the party concerned is unlikely to hear it.

'Publish and be damned' is an honourable position, at least in theory. But again I must emphasise that even the consumer area, where radio stations often, rightly, play the role of the consumer's champion, is fraught with dangers. There is perhaps more leeway here than in other areas, but you and your production team have got to be absolutely clear about what is likely to provoke legal action.

Who can sue?

It will have become apparent that almost anyone can sue. Not just adult individuals and children but also companies. They can sue if a libel has affected their trading or business. But remember that individuals working in a company can sue in their own right.

Local authorities can no longer sue for libel though, again, it's important to remember that individual officers could sue if they are identifiable.

There is no libel of the dead though a defamatory statement about a dead person may impinge upon the reputation of a living relative, so be careful.

Other matters relating to defamation

Repetition

Repetition of a libel is considered a fresh libel and actionable as such. Be careful, then, when using newspaper reports to provoke phone-in arguments. Just because a story has been through a newspaper's lawyers doesn't mean to say that it isn't actionable.

Innuendo

It is possible to libel someone by using language which might be incomprehensible to one set of people and understandable to those 'in the know'. So 'encoding' a comment is no defence against legal action. This is well illustrated by the case of former cabinet minister Lord Gowrie. He received damages after suing the *Star* newspaper over an article which suggested, without actually saying so, that he took drugs. The article referred to his 'expensive habits' and said that Lord Gowrie would 'snort at suggestions that he was born with a silver spoon round his neck'. Lord Gowrie's counsel said that to anyone familiar with all the terminology, the implication was that he was in the habit of taking illegal drugs.

'General' allegations

You may often be tempted to make a remark such as 'all estate agents are crooks'. This probably falls outside the law of defamation. However, you could not legally get away with saying the same about all estate agents on Leicester High Street. The point is that it is possible to defame a group of people if each member of the group could successfully claim that a story had been 'reasonably understood to refer to him or her'. It all depends on how large the group is. What is a 'safe' number? Impossible to say! You and your producer must tread carefully.

Naming names

As will have become clear, you don't have to name names to provide someone with an opportunity for suing for defamation. Individuals have often sued who have been the victim of the so-called 'jig-saw effect'. This means that although someone is not directly identified, if their identity is suggested or implied by a number of details in what is said, they can indeed sue. So even talking in veiled terms about an individual or a company is potentially dangerous.

What to do if you think a libel is broadcast

As I've said above, dealing with libel 'as it happens' is not easy. Over time, you should develop a sixth sense concerning the possibility of a caller or guest uttering something defamatory. If it starts to happen, interrupt or cut your contributor off. If, in spite of your best efforts, your contributor continues, it's a good idea to disassociate the station from the comments made. Use some such phrase as: 'Those, I must immediately say, are not the views of Radio X.' This won't necessarily prevent a libel action, but at least it will show good will on the part of the station.

The law of contempt

The law of contempt is there to ensure that the course of justice is not impeded, perverted or in any other way interfered with. In general terms, this means that broadcasters have to ensure that reporting and comment do not prejudice the outcome of court cases or influence people who have to make decisions in court – in particular, the jury.

As with defamation, callers and interviewees often have scant knowledge of the law in this area. Indeed, because we are more aware now of the way in which some American court cases have become a species of TV entertainment, the sense has grown that anyone can say anything about a court case which is in progress.

The gravity of breaking the law of contempt is well illustrated in the following case study.

Case study

This relates to the Harold Shipman trial which took place early in the year 2000. Dr Shipman was accused of murdering a number of his patients.

A presenter at a Northern English radio station and the traffic reporter had a conversation on air about Dr Shipman and the trial which was then in progress.

In the broadcast the presenter was reported as saying: 'The Harold Shipman trial . . . we've got to be delicate here because it's ongoing . . . I'm supposed to be delicate, but really I don't care. Harold Shipman's trial is going into its umpteen month. . . ' At this point, the traffic reporter was heard to say: 'Guilty.' The presenter continued: ' . . . innocent until proven guilty, of course, because that's the way it works in this land. It's innocent until proven guilty as sin. Put us tax payers out of our misery, because we're paying for this. Admit to it, it's a fair cop, you're caught red-handed, be done with it.'

The trial Judge heard a tape of the broadcast and ordered them both to attend court. He said: 'In my view, this was about as irresponsible a piece of broadcasting as I have heard.' He made clear that he thought the remarks were calculated to prejudice the fairness of the trial and hence, in his preliminary view, they represented 'blatant contempt of court'.

Both narrowly escaped being sent to jail only because of the quality of the management of the station's MD, in the way she had dealt with the broadcast and because the jury did not hear the broadcast.

The Judge commented: 'You did something that could have resulted in this trial being restarted before a fresh jury.'

Shipman was later found guilty and is now regarded as the biggest mass murderer that the United Kingdom has ever experienced.

This case demonstrates just how seriously the courts take contempt. Something like the conversation of the presenter and traffic reporter could doubtless have been heard in pubs and sitting rooms across the land throughout the trial. But they made their remarks on air, so they immediately became prejudicial. Presenters must be as aware of the law of contempt as of that of defamation and seek to prevent callers and guests from breaking the law.

When does the law of contempt apply?

The law of contempt applies when cases are 'active'. Criminal proceedings become active at one of these four points:

- When someone is arrested.
- When someone is charged orally.
- When a warrant for arrest is issued.
- When a summons is issued.

Often, broadcasters don't know when the active period has started. But under the law they are 'strictly liable' which means that ignorance is no defence.

A civil case becomes active when it is set down for trial in County Court, that is when a date is fixed for the hearing.

Journalists who are reporting on active cases have to tread a very fine line so as not to break the contempt laws. If you want to go into this more deeply, then you should consult one of the standard texts mentioned above But as a presenter you must be very careful about what you, your guests and callers say about active cases.

In general, you should not discuss material which could affect the outcome of a case. This means, amongst other things, that you should not, during the active period:

- broadcast an interview with a witness or a juror
- speculate about the outcome of a case
- comment on a case due for retrial
- repeat what is said in the absence of a jury.

Defences against contempt

The Producers' Guidelines published by the BBC sum up very well how little room for manoeuvre broadcasters have:

> The defence of public interest is of very limited value in cases of contempt. Judges may overlook minor or unintentional acts. They may also resist attempts by third parties to use contempt as a means of preventing the broadcasting of material of proper interest to the public.
>
> There is a statutory right to provide a fair, accurate and contemporaneous account of court proceedings held in public, but this right is qualified. Judges have the freedom to postpone the reporting of an entire case or certain details of it.

There is, then, very little defence against a charge of contempt. The golden rule has to be that in a general talk programme you should steer clear of any comment on a case which is active. If in doubt, say nowt!

Conclusion

I hope it will have become clear that whereas the law relating to contempt is relatively straightforward and leaves little or no room for comment on cases which are active, the law relating to defamation is a lot more grey because it is open to interpretation. In consumer phone-ins especially, if you as a presenter applied the letter of the law the resultant broadcast would sound bland. On the other hand, if you let callers simply say what they like about firms providing goods and services your station could get into serious trouble.

As with a lot of things covered in this book, experience has got to be the teacher. But even having said that, you should always err on the side of caution. Remember, it will be the station which is sued if it publishes a libel. The management will not look smilingly on you if they start to receive solicitors' letters as a result of what you have said. An on-air misjudgement in these areas of the law could cost you your contract and your professional reputation.

Tutorial

1. What is libel?
2. What is slander?
3. What is contempt?
4. What is meant by repetition of a libel?
5. What are the defences to libel in English Law?

Seminar discussion

1. The purpose of the law of contempt is to ensure that justice is not compromised by careless infringements from the ignorant, ill-informed, malicious or just plain stupid. However, in the USA the public have the right to know. Should we have a similar right to know in the UK and if so, what would be the implications for the Shipman trial contempt mentioned above?

Practical assignments

1. Contact the County Court in your area and sit in on a case, in the public gallery. Make sure you do not record anything you hear in the court but listen intently and form your own view of the nature of the justice system, either here in the UK or where you live.

6

Expect the Unexpected

One-minute summary – Broadcasters need to be secure people who can cope with stress because radio studios can be very stressful.
In this chapter you will learn:

- the different pressures that a broadcaster has to deal with
- the nature of the everyday pressures facing a broadcaster in the studio
- how to keep the right tone in untoward events.

Control

You might recall that a few years ago the nation voted as its favourite poem Rudyard Kipling's 'If'. This uplifting piece of verse begins:

> If you can keep your head when all about you
> Are losing theirs and blaming it on you . . .

And it ends, having listed many bracing character traits:

> Yours is the Earth and everything that's in it,
> And – what is more – you'll be a Man, my son!

Setting aside the sexism of the poem (presumably women have no need of the qualities of character which make men men) it does sum up rather well at least one of the attributes of a good presenter – man or women: you must always keep your head even when all about you are indeed losing theirs. All sorts of mayhem and chaos may break out in the studio, but the moment panic creeps into your voice listeners will realise you are not in control and the professionalism, so valued by the radio audience, will have melted away.

Julian Worricker of 5 Live made the point to me that listeners spot even tiny things which indicate that a presenter is not on top of things. He says: 'It is vital to remain calm on-air at all times. I know I tend to speed up if things get a little tense, and now consciously slow myself down in such circumstances. I guess I'm lucky to be a fairly relaxed person in the studio – a colleague of mine once suggested I had valium instead of blood.'

Julian's point is that you must be aware of how you sound at all times and consciously adjust your performance if you feel yourself losing control. However, this does not mean that you should lack passion or be afraid of spontaneity. Especially in a phone-in, but also in interviews, passion, enthusiasm, anger, even, are all vital. But such emotions should never get in the way of a professional performance.

So what are the pressures of presenting a live talk sequence? These can be divided into two:

- Everyday pressure.
- Out of the ordinary pressure.

Everyday pressure

These pressures are so basic that if you can't handle them with aplomb you had better find another career. They boil down to the fact that at any one time on air you will have to be thinking of several things at the same time.

As an example, let us suppose you are conducting a live interview with someone in the studio. This is with a local councillor about proposals to redevelop a part of the town which will entail the demolition of well-used public amenities and a number of well-loved buildings. You start the interview at 22 minutes past the hour and you know that at 30 minutes past the hour you have a down-the-line interview with a popular TV personality. She is available for only ten minutes but she will add much needed sparkle to the programme.

As you embark upon your first interview you will be aware that you have got to put as many questions about the implications of the redevelopment plan as possible without sounding superficial. At some point you might decide to lose a few minutes from the beginning of your next interview for the sake of extracting from the councillor the admission that this is at least a controversial plan, at worst a disastrous one. So as you are listening to what he says, formulating your questions, preparing yourself for the next interview, you are also keeping an eye on the studio clock and, of course, listening to your producer. He or she will probably be the ultimate arbiter on when one interview ends and the other begins. Nevertheless, it has been known for presenters to over-ride producers if they think what is going on now is of more significance that what is coming up in a few minutes!

It will always be the case that as you are doing one interview you will be preparing for what is coming after, whether it be another interview, a disc, the news, a weather check or some phone calls. There will always be fixed junctions to meet (news, traffic reports, weather etc) and these should become second nature to you. You might have to 'spin out' an interview to get up to a junction or curtail one as naturally as you can.

And there will always be the unexpected interview which you will have to do without cue or preparation. If your producer is on his or her toes, the programme will have various items which are responses to the day's local and national news. These will be 'jacked up' whilst the programme is on air and filtered in, often at very short notice, as and when the interviewee becomes available.

Your producer will be communicating with you through headphones and by means of messages on your VDU. Most presenters also like to keep an eye on breaking news as it comes in from the agencies and on television ceefax.

Today's presenters are bombarded with information. They must be able to sort out the important stuff from the unimportant and so keep a sense of proper priorities. They must keep one step ahead of the game whilst at the same time talking challengingly or charmingly to callers and guests.

In my experience none of this gets any easier as you get older and the grey cells begin to decay. As I write this I am in my 50th year and keeping a programme on the right tracks is more difficult now than 20 years ago. However, let me not depress you . . . or come to that, me. The pressure of spontaneous, live radio is part of its pleasure. At the end of a lively programme which has gone well you should feel a glow of satisfaction and achievement. Any presenter will tell you that spending three hours on-air is quite tiring. But there is all the difference in the world between the exhilarated tiredness which comes after three hours which have sped past, and the tiredness born of panic after a programme seems to have been on-air forever.

If you find yourself experiencing too many of the latter you and your producer must sit down and analyse the reasons. It is more than possible that you are not getting the proper back-up. If you producer is not on the ball or is not communicating with you properly during the programme then this will put you under unnecessary pressure.

As I've said before, a good, professional relationship between a producer and a presenter is vital. In many cases the problems experienced by a presenter should be solved at a programme post-mortem meeting. If you feel you can't say what needs saying for the success of the programme something is wrong with the relationship.

Out of the ordinary pressures

The second kind of pressure should not be run of the mill. Sometimes this kind of pressure is exhilarating, sometimes it will mean you have got to use all of your professionalism to 'cover up the cracks'.

Let's take the second kind first. Radio is a highly technical medium and as it has become more sophisticated and complicated it's also become (at least in my experience) more prone to things going wrong. So, inserts from radio cars go dead mid-sentence; a guest in a remote studio can hear you, but you can't hear him; the station's phone-lines suddenly elect not to work, etc, etc. In each of these cases the presenter can't fix the problem. He or she has simply got to carry on whilst those who can sort out the problem do so.

Ideally, you should have an emergency item to go to if necessary. Always have a station ident or public service announcement waiting to be played. This will buy valuable time. I like to have one, usually frivolous, talking point up my sleeve which I haven't mentioned before. This gives you the opportunity to chat for two or three minutes whilst, hopefully, the problem is ironed out.

In fact, you should be able to chat about this and that for a few minutes on many subjects of current and general interest – the monologue should be part of your stock-in-trade. During a lull in one programme (I don't recall the reason) I found myself chuntering on about old fashioned ice-cream and its superiority to the modern stuff. I still don't quite know why this sparkling topic came into my mind but it did the trick. Soon we were inundated with calls on the great ice-cream debate and the hiatus was comfortably covered.

Human error

Sometimes, of course, a problem is not technical but human. Even after all the years I've spent working in radio I'm still surprised at the fact that some guests simply don't turn up. When later contacted, many are quite unapologetic and feel that having had something better to do was explanation enough for their non-appearance. The fact that they might have inconvenienced someone seems not to have occurred to them.

Admittedly such banes of the broadcasters life are few. But only a couple of months ago the programme on which I work was confronted with the fact that two consecutive guests failed to arrive. This, of course, represented a big chunk of the programme and caused no little difficulty. The problem was compounded by the fact that we were having a slow day on the phones so there was no question of using calls to fill the gap.

I did a monologue on something of local interest, the producer dropped in to preview some specialist phone-ins over the coming weeks, I played one more piece of music than I should have, read the events diary at great length . . . somehow we papered over the crack.

I was amazed when I discovered that no one in the production office had noticed that there had been a problem. But then, the secret is to make everything sound as though it has been preplanned and a natural part of the programme.

Dealing with events

The other kind of pressure comes from *events* which demand to be covered at short notice. Three very different examples come to mind.

Firstly, there was the resignation of Margaret Thatcher. This was, to use the old cliché but justified in this case, the end of an era. It was all anyone wanted to talk about and so on the programme I present we simply cancelled all our guests and filled the three hours with phone-calls, phone-outs to MPs, academic experts, historians and anyone with something useful or important to say on the subject of her years in power. This meant a huge amount of improvisation for producer and presenter alike. As I started one interview I usually had no idea to whom I would be speaking next or when. There was no time for well-turned cues and carefully thought out questions: the programme was made up as we went along.

In such a case you have to draw on all your accumulated political knowledge. Without such knowledge and a sense of the right questions to ask a programme like that would simply fall apart.

A comparable occasion was the death of the much respected Labour leader John Smith. Obviously Smith was not nearly so significant a figure as Margaret Thatcher, but his unexpected death at a time when he was slowly reinventing the Labour Party to make it more electable raised all sorts of questions about the future of Westminster politics.

Clearing the decks

Again we 'cleared the decks' and improvised a programme consisting of tribute and analysis of his legacy. And again such a programme would not have been possible without an ability to keep on asking the relevant questions with little in the way of on-air back-up: the producer was too busy finding other guests.

Although the death of John Smith was very sad, both that programme and the one following Margaret Thatcher's resignation were, in their own ways, exhilarating. They set real challenges and surmounting them successfully provided a real sense of achievement for everyone involved.

The death of Diana, Princess of Wales

The third 'bolt from the blue' set its own challenges, but for the production team the feelings involved were anything but exhilarating. This was the death of Diana, Princess of Wales. The week between her death and her funeral was an extremely difficult one for all sorts of reasons. Feelings in the country were running high anyway, but there was the unmistakeable sense that some sections of the press were orchestrating the public's emotions in a cynical way.

On air, we wanted to reflect the real sense of loss that people naturally felt. But other voices were clamouring to be heard, not least the conspiracy theorists; those who wanted to point out, quite forcefully in some cases, that the Princess wasn't the saint she was being portrayed as; those who felt that anything other than reverent sorrow was somehow an insult, not just to royalty, but a threat to the nation at large.

Trying to allow all these voices to be heard at the same time as not offending the genuine sense of loss felt by many people was extremely difficult. I certainly thought that the tabloids were milking the occasion in an unseemly way and said so. This provoked those who saw the papers as simply reflecting what most people felt. In that week's unreal atmosphere people took offence easily, heard slights where none were intended and made presenting those five programmes very problematic.

Our aim, which the production team spoke about at length, was to maintain a proper dignity, whilst allowing all but the most gratuitously unpleasant to have their say. Those with 'unorthodox' views were challenged, but they were heard. I think we held the line, but it wasn't easy.

Tone

In each of the three cases mentioned, maintaining an appropriate *tone* was vital. The resignation of Margaret Thatcher and the deaths of John Smith and Diana, Princess of Wales, were all significant political, historical or social turning points. They needed a tone of some gravity but (especially the first two) they also required analysis and some dispassionate commentary.

A sense of appropriate tone, like so much else, is something which must become second nature to you. You won't just need this for big national events such as the ones I've mentioned above. The death of a local politician, or of a regular caller will require you to say appropriate words and sense when someone is perhaps straying into inappropriate tones and areas.

Nothing antagonises a listener more than a feeling that a presenter is adopting a tone of inappropriate levity. But equally, listening to three hours of sonorous gravitas is hardly a recipe for riveting listening.

Tutorial

1. What is meant by the phrase 'appropriate tone'?
2. Prepare a monologue on a topic that you could talk about for 2 minutes.

Seminar discussion

Disasters will always happen but there are certain things professional broadcasters can do. For instance, it is possible to identify celebrities and important people who are aged and clearly are in the autumn of their years. When a death then occurs, it is possible to present pre-prepared material on air. Is this practice ethical?

Practical assignments

1. Identify at least two notable achievers in your area, eg a long serving councillor/local representative. Use the local press cuttings, usually held in the local library, to create a profile of that person, to go on file. Identify contacts who could be brought in to comment on your subject's achievements. Do not contact them or your subject.

2. Identify notable national achievers who have a local connection to your area and repeat the practice above.

7

Local Radio, Past, Present and Future

One-minute summary – For the duration of a brief chapter we turn aside from practical matters to look at something of the history of local radio in this country. It is important that you understand the development of the medium in which you aspire to work.

In this chapter you will learn:

- how local radio began in the UK
- the nature of radio and how the industry is changing.

Radio doesn't exist in a timeless present. It has its own distinct traditions and history and these affect the way it is likely to develop in the future. To understand what's going on now you need to have a grasp of what went on in the past. But in any case, if you are genuinely interested in the medium, part of that interest is almost certainly going to be in its unfolding story.

Origins

It is sometimes forgotten that radio was, in its origins, a local medium. The first radio services were broadcast from Birmingham, Manchester and Newcastle in 1922. As the most recent charter for BBC local radio puts it: 'the very foundation of the BBC was local, not national, broadcasting'. Within a short time stations were opening across the country, but these were soon closed down and the BBC, whilst maintaining a regional structure, became based in London.

However, the story of modern local radio in this country starts in 1967. It was the brain-child of one of the Corporation's most distinguished war correspondents, Frank Gillard. After the war Gillard moved into management and in 1963 he was appointed Director of Sound Broadcasting.

Visits to America left him fascinated by the way local radio worked over there. In particular, he liked the way the stations reflected and provided a focus for often quite small communities. He became convinced that the BBC should start its own comprehensive local radio service. However, he didn't want to impose the American model of programming lock, stock and barrel in Britain. The American stations were an inspiration, not a template. As Asa Briggs, the historian of broadcasting, has written: 'The object of local radio, Gillard insisted, was not to set up "amplified juke boxes", but to offer "modern radio journalism" geared to the interests of the local community.'

Technical developments in the 1950s made Gillard's vision a possibility. The introduction of VHF frequencies provided an expansion of airwaves so technically there was no reason why local radio shouldn't be established. But there was a marked reluctance on the part of the BBC hierarchy to entertain the idea.

In 1997, at a dinner to celebrate 30 years of local radio, Frank Gillard made a moving speech about how he fought to get his idea turned into reality. He held numerous meetings with local authorities who might be interested in 'playing host' to a radio station and generally, according to his account, made himself unpopular with the BBC hierarchy by arguing his case at every available opportunity.

Finally, in 1966, the BBC submitted a plan for local radio which was later incorporated into a White Paper. This said:

> The local radio station will provide the missing link of communication. Day after day, it will be talking to the citizens about their town, bringing them into contact with each other, engaging their interest and participation, telling the running story of local life and building the satisfying and rewarding sense of the larger town family.

Those words still provide an excellent summary of what BBC local radio and some ILR stations attempt to do. Frank Gillard summed up the aspirations of local radio even more succinctly: 'Local radio will provide a running serial of local life in all its aspects, involving a multitude of local voices; what one might call the people's radio.'

Gillard finally saw his vision of what he called 'home town radio' realised on Wednesday November 8th, when BBC Radio Leicester, the first modern local radio station, came on the air at 12.45pm with a message delivered by the Postmaster General, Edward Short.

The idea of local radio was not met with universal acclamation. On that first day, there were protests outside the building in which Radio Leicester was housed from those who objected to the outlawing of the pirate radio stations operating from ships moored in the North Sea. Moreover, there was a plan for the local authority to part-fund the station and many business people, to say nothing of ordinary rate-payers, objected to this.

For many years BBC local radio was very much the Cinderella of the Corporation. Whenever there was a budget crisis the local radio chain came under threat. Often local radio escaped closure apparently by the skin of its teeth. But survive it did, and it gradually changed and developed.

Developments

The early broadcasts of that pioneering station were very different from those of BBC local stations today. For a start, Leicester only originated less than four hours of original material a day, the rest of the time the station relayed programmes from the newly re-branded network stations. (On September 30th 1967 the old Light Programme, Third Programme and Home Service were redesignated Radios 2, 3 and 4. A new network, Radio 1, was opened on the same day). The programmes that were originated in Leicester were rather formal in their presentational style and were modelled on what could be heard on Radio 4. Most focused on a particular subject or topic (local industry, politics, religion etc) and they were generally half an hour or an hour in length.

Quite early on Radio Leicester broadcast the first phone-in. This was on the gardening programme hosted by Geoff Amos, one of the first local people to be recruited by the new station to present and appear in specialist programmes. Geoff remembers:

> It was certainly the first phone-in on local radio. The producer, Ken Warburton, had the idea and our station engineer, Martin Lane, devised the necessary technology. This was only two or three months after we went on-air and it was a completely novel idea. We had no idea whether it would work and I certainly had doubts about it. I thought I'd be sitting there with a couple of gardeners and there'd be no questions for us, so I devised a list of questions in case nobody called. When people did begin to call it was a very pleasant surprise. I was amazed at the number who did call in during that first programme. I didn't have to use any of my stand-by questions! After that we ran a fortnightly phone-in on our gardeners' programme and of course other programmes on the station soon latched on to the idea. But I think it was some time before other stations realised its potential. Looking back on it and realising how important the phone-in is to radio these days, that first use of it on my programme was an historic occasion!

The phone-in has, of course, become a staple element in local radio's output, making every listener a potential broadcaster and guaranteeing local involvement. If there is one thing which has given local and national speech-based radio its flavour and distinctiveness it's the phone-in which allows the community to talk to itself.

Right from the outset local radio came into its own in times of crisis. During the first winter that Radio Leicester was on the air there were bad floods in the city centre. The new station was able to provide up-to-the-minute reports about the situation and in so doing gained many new listeners. It was able to cover the crisis in a way that no other medium could. Since then when the weather has caused havoc, when blizzards have struck or when power lines have gone down local radio has proved itself a lifeline for the community it serves. Since 1990, many stations have been given the official role of providing the vital link between emergency services and residents in distress.

Manchester and the IRA

There are many examples of the way local radio can provide essential help in a crisis. Here are two. In 1996 Manchester was rocked by a huge IRA bomb explosion. Radio GMR's coverage of the aftermath of the explosion won a Sony award for the quality of its reporting. The round-the-clock information the station was able to broadcast was an essential part of the process by which the city came to terms with what had happened. The autumn floods of 2000 also brought out the best in the stations in the areas worst affected. Their coverage won plaudits from the Deputy Prime Minister, who wrote a letter of thanks to the BBC: 'The weather conditions have obviously caused a great deal of distress. But the up-to-date information provided by local media has kept people informed and allowed people to plan ahead.' Mr Prescott was 'particularly struck' by the efforts of a BBC journalist, Victoria Green, in York. He met her covering the plight of householders in Malton. 'As well as reporting on the floods, [she] was helping people to move furniture and other valuables to safety. Truly an example of a radio station at the heart of the community, and reproduced in many other areas.'

Within months of the opening of Radio Leicester seven other local radio stations were on air, followed, in 1969, by twelve more. In the 1980s the local radio 'chain' was complete: 38 stations now reach over 90% of the population.

The 'sound' of local radio, its style of broadcasting gradually evolved. The old discreet programmes gave way to the 'sequence'. This is a three or even four hour stretch of broadcasting covering a wide variety of subjects and approaches, the whole thing given focus and shape by a single presenter.

This soon became the pattern for all BBC local radio stations and it remains the pattern today. Local people relate to 'their' presenters: they like 'personality' broadcasting, access and a friendly, informal style. The sequence, well produced and presented, can provide all these things.

Originally, station managers had considerable freedom and they found their own ways to reflect the community their stations served. I remember in the early 80s as I travelled the country marvelling at how different the BBC's stations sounded. The impact of competition saw a diminution of autonomy in the 1990s. Various charters and directives moulded the stations into a chain whose distinctiveness lay in its speech-based programming and journalism. This did not (and does not) mean that they all sounded the same. Each station has a distinct identity because it has its own presenters and reflects a unique locality.

Competition

The BBC has never had a radio monopoly. Radio Luxembourg and then the 'pirates' of the 1960s prompted the BBC to change. Radio 1 came about as a direct result of this 'unofficial' opposition. Then, in 1973, the first commercial stations went on air: LBC closely followed by Capital Radio.

The latest charter for BBC local radio remarks: 'Paradoxically, it was the very success of BBC Local Radio in the late sixties that fuelled the debate and provided ammunition for the commercial lobby which demanded frequencies on a spectrum liberated by VHF, particularly at the local level'.

Indeed, many of the early stations which aimed to provide predominantly speech-based programmes were heavily influenced by the BBC local radio style. But the 1990 Broadcasting Act, as well as establishing a new regulator, the Radio Authority, removed many of the public service obligations from ILR. This has resulted in the huge range of formats you can hear today. ILR is now music dominated and although some of its stations make speech their basis, the main provider of speech-based radio remains BBC local radio. This is an important niche in the market but the extent of the success of competition can be gauged by the fact that at the beginning of the new millennium commercial radio has overtaken the BBC with a 50.6% share of listening.

Local radio is increasingly important to the BBC for a number of reasons. It clearly provides a popular service to a large audience. Listener satisfaction is remarkably high: it comes second only to BBC1 in BBC services most valued by listeners and viewers. BBC local radio appeals to an important section of the population: its core audience is 50+. This actually means that in most places

BBC local radio co-exists with rather than competes with ILR stations which tend to have a music-liking 15-24 audience. The local radio chain also acts as a very efficient news gathering service with BBC journalists and studios all over the country.

As I write, BBC local radio seems very secure for these and other reasons. The new charter for local radio reaffirms the value the BBC places on this part of its service. Local radio stations will remain rooted in their communities yet firmly a part of the Corporation.

The future and narrowcasting

BBC local radio thinks of itself as a *broad*caster. It treats a wide range of subjects and aims to appeal to a wide range of people within its target audience. Listen to any of the stations' mid-morning programmes and you'll probably hear consumer items, author interviews, features on local history, interviews with councillors and council officers, charity workers, musicians, actors, cooks...

Independent Local Radio has gone down the route of *narrow*casting. The stations aim to target a very specific audience and provide them, day in and day out, with material which meets their particular interest whether it be sport, jazz, dance, 'gold' music, output for ethnic communities etc.

This fragmentation of the market is in line with the watchword 'choice' which governed so much of public life and political decision making in the 1990s. It seems clear that we will see more and more local stations, some of them covering a very small area indeed. The most successful of these have a predominantly music format but still sound local and community based. Examples are Oak FM in Loughborough and Spire FM in Salisbury. These will doubtless be the pattern and model for more and more stations.

But regional stations will also have a future. They have proved popular in the North East, North West and East Midlands. The Radio Authority will be granting more regional licences in the near future.

There are over 200 ILR stations operating at present and there will be many more to come. It seems likely that as many licences will be issued as the market can stand. The development of digital broadcasting allows for an almost limitless number of stations. Already stations are targeting communities within their editorial areas by simulcasting two or three versions of their news bulletins and breakfast programmes. As well as more local 'grassroots' broadcasting, digital technology will soon offer multimedia radio with text, pictures and interactivity. The impact and implications of the digital age are still to be fully understood.

Meanwhile the BBC itself is planning five new national radio services that will be available through digital formats. These include the Asian Network presently available to only a limited audience.

At present, BBC local radio, whilst having to adapt to the huge increase in competition and the impact of digital developments, still retains the affection of the older, heart-land audience. But there is no guarantee that this situation will continue. Soon some ILR stations will begin to target the 50 year old + audience with a service comparable to that provided by the BBC. SAGA radio is now operating as a prime time radio service and broadcasting to the 50 year old + audience which has traditionally sustained BBC local radio, in the English Midlands regional radio franchise. They will be challenging for the BBC local radio audience.

The proliferation of stations is, of course, good news for potential presenters. Opportunities abound, but to keep abreast of what is happening you must listen to as many stations as possible and read the trade press. Only if you know what is going on will you have the knowledge to apply successfully for jobs and tailor your performance to what is required.

Tutorial

1. Where was the first local radio station in the UK?
2. What was Frank Gillard's role in the development of UK local radio?

Seminar discussion

The current developments in digital radio show how the market is

fragmenting. 6Music and One Extra are examples of new radio stations that are only available on digital frequencies.
Is there a role for a digital station catering for people over the age of 50?
If so why?
If not, why not?

Practical assignments

Using a digital receiver or a satellite TV receiver, listen to at least two digital stations that are not available via analogue receivers. Analyse the programmes and the presenter style. Look to see if they have a gap in their programming schedule that you could fill as a presenter.

8

Life as a Freelancer

One-minute summary – In this chapter we are concerned with looking after and controlling your income. You will need to think about five main areas:

- tax
- pensions
- sickness
- holidays
- National Insurance.

Freelancing: the agonies and the ecstasies

The number of staff radio presenters in this country is tiny. Overwhelmingly, presenters work to short-term, usually a year, contracts or on a programme to programme or series to series basis.

This means that managing your career is not just a question of turning up to fulfill your contract. Being a successful freelance entails considerable work outside the studio. Some of this is mundane (filling out tax forms etc.), but making a go of being a freelance can be a fulfilling experience.

Freelancing, it hardly needs saying, is not a secure business. If you don't enjoy taking risks and so worry a lot about where your career will be in a year's time (or indeed whether you will *have* a career then), you will either have to conquer your worries or think about working in a more secure industry.

I can say this with some authority. I became a full-time freelance having been a teacher for almost 15 years. Teaching is a real career. It has a structure and, of course, as an employee of a local authority, such matters as income tax, holiday pay, National Insurance and so on, are all taken care of for you.

My decision to change careers was not an easy one. I recognised that it would be a case of sink or swim, that I couldn't count on a steadily increasing income and that I might remain a 'hack' broadcaster for the rest of my working life.

Over a decade later I have never regretted the decision to change horses. Although I am a bit of a worrier, I soon realised that no job these days, staff or otherwise, is secure. And as soon as I began to get work outside the local radio station which provided me with my main income I began to feel more confident that life as a freelance was exciting and rewarding.

However, before we look at those rewards, let's examine the basics of managing a freelance career.

Tax

The easiest way to deal with the Inland Revenue is to pay someone to do this for you: an accountant. And the best way of finding someone reliable is by asking around. Find out who friends and colleagues use. Personal recommendation is always the best way of finding someone who will deal properly with your financial affairs. The Institute of Chartered Accountants in England and Wales can also provide you with names of Chartered Accountants. Their telephone number is 01536 500850.

Your accountant will be able to provide useful advice on what purchases you can and cannot claim against income tax. He or she will compile your annual tax return and generally look after your tax affairs. Your accountant's fee is chargeable against tax and if you find filling in forms and keeping up with the latest pronouncements of the Chancellor of the Exchequer a bore, then investigate this possibility.

But be warned. Hiring an accountant does not absolve you from keeping your financial records in good order. You must keep the bills of everything you purchase which you think can be off-set against income tax and, of course, all records of earnings from whatever source.

None of this is difficult. It's very easy simply to have a file or even a large envelope into which you can put all your records as a matter of course. Then once a year, sort them out and send them off to your accountant. He or she will take care of the rest of the process. Your accountant will wish to see you before the tax return is finally completed. This meeting is always a good opportunity for you to consult him or her about developments on the tax front and for them to advise you on relevant matters.

You may well think that your accountant's fee is money well spent for a chore you don't want to do yourself. On the other hand, the new self-assessment forms issued by the Inland Revenue are not that difficult to fill in. You can save yourself some money simply by doing it yourself.

However you deal with tax matters you cannot afford to be slap-dash about this area of your finances. You must keep your receipts, records of payment in good order and ensure that everything required by the Revenue is submitted in good time.

It is also important that you make regular savings towards your tax bill which is generally collected twice a year. You will soon get a sense of what your annual earnings will be. Work out roughly what your tax bill will be, divide by 12 and put that sum into a savings account on a monthly basis. Search around for an account which best suits your needs and pays reasonable interest on your savings. You need to be aware that you probably will have to pay your tax **in advance**. In the UK, freelancers are required to pay tax on account, this means they need to pay tax before they have earned the money. There are exceptions to this so do take professional advice.

Pensions

Retirement may seem a very long way off. But unless you start planning for it from the start of your career you could find yourself having to cope with a financially straitened old age.

The problem is that there are now so many different pension plans on the market that it is almost impossible for the uninitiated to make an advantageous choice. In my experience, an independent financial adviser is the most useful person you will engage to help run the financial side of your career. A cooperative adviser will keep tabs on all your savings and investment needs, arrange for an annual interview so that you can be appraised of your situation and generally keep you on the financial straight and narrow.

Everyone who works in the radio industry has different financial needs and simply being able to discuss in detail your financial position with someone who knows the subject is always fruitful.

As with accountants, some IFAs are more efficient than others. Again, the best way to find one is through personal recommendation. IFA Promotions will also be able to help you by providing a list of local registered advisers. Their phone number is 0117 9711177.

Sickness

Even if you work as a contract freelance it is highly unlikely that it will have provision for payment if sickness prevents you from working. It follows that *you* must make provision for this eventuality.

You can, of course, take out insurance against this and I would strongly advise that you investigate products which are on the market with your IFA. But be warned. Almost all of these policies only begin to yield payment after you have been off work for a month. Illness can strike at any time and if you are forced to take off only two or three days because of a cold or throat infection this can make a big difference to your financial position and plans. So it is a good idea to build up a sum of money to help fund illness. This will need to be kept in a reasonably liquid savings account because you may need your money at short notice. Again, talk to your IFA about finding a savings account which best suits your needs.

Holiday pay

As with sickness pay, your contract will probably not yield holiday pay, though it will doubtless stipulate how much time you can have off for your holidays. If you don't work you won't get paid. So make sure that you save regularly for four or five weeks holiday a year. These savings can be paid into the account you use for illness cover.

National Insurance

You would be advised to pay your National Insurance contributions by direct debit. To organise this, simply contact the Inland Revenue Contributions Office at the following address:

Self Employment Directorate
Longbenton
Newcastle Upon Tyne
NE98 1YX

You will need your NI number when you make your arrangements. It's also vital to tell the office if your circumstances change whether it be your home address, phone number or if you cease to be self-employed.

Yes, I know! Financial matters can seem irrelevant and not a little tedious. But taking care of your money matters is vital. You never know when you will become ill, you *must* take holidays or you will become terminally stressed, the tax man is always on the prowl and one day you will retire and you will need an adequate income. For all of these reasons you need to plan now. And the best people to help you plan, unless you really are clued up in these areas, are a good accountant and IFA.

Developing your freelance work

If you work to a contract your staple income will come from the station for which you regularly work. But you can develop your career in all sorts of areas once you have become established.

Working for other stations

If you work for an ILR station your contract will certainly prevent you from working for competitors. However, if you work for a BBC local station there will probably be no bar to your working for other stations in the chain and for network stations.

Working for network stations can be a useful source of income if you have the interests and skills needed by them. BBC Radio 4, especially, commissions dozens of programme series every year and its producers are always on the look-out for fresh ideas.

Contact your nearest network centre and find out who produces what. Make an appointment and pitch some ideas. Experienced producers know what the network is looking for and will be able to develop your ideas into submissions to commissioning editors. You might not be lucky, but if you are and the programme or series is well received you should soon get established as a reliable network presenter.

Over the past ten years I've presented dozens of series and 'one-offs' for Radios 2 and 4. Some of these have been my own ideas, others the ideas of producers who have liked my work and approached me to front the programmes. I've gone for long periods with no network work, at other times the offers have come thick and fast. Whatever the case you will only be successful if you keep coming up with saleable ideas. So listen carefully to the station you want to work for, maintain contact with producers . . . network . . . put yourself about! Make sure they are aware of your abilities and that you can deliver what they want.

Videos/voice overs

Many presenters voice corporate, local history and other videos. Once your voice has become well known in your locality you will probably be approached to do this sort of work. But you can easily make a pre-emptive strike. Every town of any size now has its independent production companies which produce tapes of this kind. Find out who they are by asking around or simply consulting *Yellow Pages*.

Contact them, go to see them and offer your voice for hire. They can only say no! Once you have done a few videos, get a show-reel professionally produced. This can be distributed to video production companies across a wide area and could get you work.

If you are extremely lucky you might even be asked to do a voice-over for a television commercial. This kind of work is extremely lucrative . . . but don't hold your breath!

Public speaking

Standing up in front of a group of people and speaking to them is a very different thing from sitting in a studio and talking into a microphone. I've known excellent broadcasters who are poor public speakers and I dare say there are good public speakers who are uninspired broadcasters. But if you do have a knack for public speaking then accept as many invitations as you can.

Over the past year I've spoken at many Women's Institutes events and to other groups, addressed a number of dinners (civic, charities, corporate), chaired public meetings and introduced more carol and other concerts than I can remember. All, to one degree or another, have been enjoyable.

On the other hand, many of them have been done for little or no fee. But then, I think that doing such jobs is an important function of the job of broadcasting. Public speaking gives you the chance to meet the people who listen to you and hear what they think of your programme and the station for which you work. Such feed-back can be useful.

Undertaking such tasks can also put you into informal contact with useful people: local and national politicians, industrialists, the Chief Constable, NHS managers, community leaders, the Bishop, the Fire Chief etc, etc. Conversation with such individuals often yields interesting information and gossip and so keeps you well informed about what's going on in your patch.

In any case, being a local presenter means more than just broadcasting. After a time you will find you have become a minor celebrity or 'personality'. People will want to see you. They want to feel that employees of 'their' station are committed enough to the audience to get out and meet them face to face.

Public speaking raises your profile and that of the station you work for; it is good PR and can provide you with useful information and contacts.

It will have become apparent that making a success of ancillary work depends on your keeping contacts alive, networking and making yourself available to do work wherever possible. Juggling a daily show, family commitments and other freelance work can be exhausting...your partner (if you have one) will have to be extremely understanding. But if you can work that juggling act the rewards can be great. And I am not necessarily talking about financial rewards. Variety is the spice of life. Presenting a programme day in day out can result in boredom. Doing other things is a great way to keep yourself and your performance fresh and bright-sounding.

Case study

Alex Trelinski has worked for 20 years in BBC and network radio. He has been a staff member, worked as a casual freelance and as a contract freelance. I asked him about how to maintain a successful freelance career.

The greatest advantage of being freelance is that it gives you flexibility: you're not tied down to one particular place or station. In the past four years I've worked on ten stations. This allows you to see what's going on, how different stations do things, how individual presenters operate and so on. All this is very interesting, keeps you on your toes and provides you with opportunities to learn. On the other hand, if you don't have a contract you do wonder where the next cheque is coming from!

To work successfully as a casual freelance you have got to be a very good broadcaster. Radio stations have only meagre freelance budgets –but they hire the best they can get in a very competitive field. But ultimately it's what you do in addition to being an excellent presenter which determines success. You have got to do a number of things. Networking is very important. Keep up your contacts, get to know as many managers and producers as you can. Sell yourself. You have got to maintain your reputation. If you screw up at one station your reputation may nose-dive. I don't just mean turning in a bad on-air performance. You've got to get on with people. You can't afford to be a prima donna. You must be helpful and cooperative at all times. After all, you're just a hired voice.

It's also good if you have a number of strings to your bow. I can do sports shifts at 5 Live and I can present general sequences on local radio stations . . . which means that you've got to adjust your style to the requirements of the station you are working on – the sequence you're presenting. Never rest on your laurels. Keep proving yourself!

It's finally worth saying that I think we are passing through a golden time for BBC local radio especially. The stations are secure, they know their audience and are responsive to it and they've got a bit more money than they had. The opportunities are there!

Tutorial

1. What is the income tax rate where you live?
2. What is 'payment on account'?
3. What are NI contributions?
4. What is an IFA?
5. What are the steps to take, to build up a pension plan?

Seminar discussion

Working as a freelancer can be stressful but it can also be extremely personally and financially rewarding. Talk this statement through with your partner. What are the implications for you and your relationship, if you become a freelancer?

Practical assignments

1. Work out a survival budget for one year. What is the minimum income you need to make, in order to survive whilst you are establishing your broadcasting career?

2. Complete a SWOT analysis, (strengths, weaknesses, opportunities, threats) for you as a freelancer. Make sure to include your vehicle. Make a critical examination of your spending habits and your potential income.

3. Create a spreadsheet and work out a cashflow forecast for yourself, as a business.

4. Complete a marketing analysis for the area where you live. How many radio stations are accessible where you live? How many independent production companies will give you the chance to record voice-overs? How many speaking engagements can you find? What are the names of the producers/managers at these companies?

5. What is your plan B? Think the worst. Imagine the scenario of giving up the day job and becoming a radio presenter to find that the move does not work out. Develop a plan to survive this unfortunate event. Do not assume this could never happen to you. This is your plan B, spend some time and think it through clearly.

9

Final Thoughts

In this chapter, you will learn:

- some common sense advice on how to survive as a professional
- the issues you need to consider for your own personal safety.

We have covered a lot of ground so far. But there remains a number of bits of advice that experience and other presenters have taught me down the years. Most are common sense, others have only really become apparent over time. All of them, I hope, will be useful.

Advice and pointers

- Drink plenty of fluids, preferably non-fizzy water. Tea and coffee can cause dryness in the throat, particularly if you do not regularly drink enough fluids, or if tea and coffee tend to be all you drink during the day. You need to lubricate your voice throughout the programme and water is the best means of doing this. Why non-fizzy? Because it might make you burp and will certainly make your stomach rumble.
- Throat clearing and coughing can both strain the vocal folds. If you feel an irritation, or a frog in your throat, sip some water.
- Eat before you go on air. Again, if you do not you could develop a stomach rumble which will make your listeners wonder where the storm is. In any case, an empty stomach is not conducive to relaxation.
- Try to walk around during news bulletins or while a long

disc is playing. Even if this is just round the studio area or along a couple of corridors, the exercise will prevent you from seizing up. Presenting is a sedentary occupation and you should get out of your chair whenever you can.

- Your voice is your fortune so you have got to take care of it. A voice specialist tells me that presenters should give up smoking, not eat too many hot or spicy meals, and avoid dry, centrally heated atmospheres. All of these can badly affect voice production.

- Get into good breathing habits. Speaking a great deal dries your throat because you breathe through your mouth when you are talking. Hence the need to drink plenty of water. Normally we breathe through the nose which starts to humidify the air before it reaches the voice box. So, because of your job, there is a danger of your becoming an habitual 'mouth breather' which could affect your voice.

- Broadcasting can be a stressful experience. In fact, stress can almost become second nature so you don't notice the tightness and tension in your muscles. There are a number of techniques for dealing with this. I have found the Alexander Technique an excellent way of reducing tension, even whilst on air. There are a number of books on this, but the only really satisfactory way of learning the technique is by going to a good teacher. Otherwise, regular exercise is a sovereign remedy for ridding yourself of the stress which inevitably goes with the job.

- Posture is important for a number of reasons. Imbalance in your posture will cause excess tension in your muscles and will therefore affect the production of your voice. Even if the excess tension is in another part of your body it will affect the muscles of the larynx. For this, and other reasons, it is important that during the time you spend on air you sit in a properly designed chair which gives proper support and is comfortable. Such a chair should support your back, be fully adjustable, allow you to rest your feet comfortably on the floor, and be completely stable, but it should not be too soft. Even if you sit on the best designed chair in the world do not tense your neck, hunch your shoulders or slump. And keep your back straight.

- Always take paper and a pen into the studio. You will always want to note something during the course of a programme.
- Ask guests wearing leather jackets and other outer wear which can creak and otherwise make distracting noises to remove them.
- Make sure that guests have turned off any mobile phones, pagers or other bits of technological jiggery-pokery which might start bleeping during the course of an interview.
- Always give out important telephone numbers, addresses, net addresses and so on more than once. The capacity of the British public not to hear these things properly, or not to have writing implements to hand, is infinite.
- Answer letters. If people take the trouble to write to you the least you can do is write back. After all, they, ultimately are the people that pay your wages and keep you on the air. There is an exception to this rule. You will inevitably receive hate mail. Usually this is sent anonymously so you will not be able to reply even if you want to. But if the writer has included an address you would be advised not to reply because this simply encourages more letters. Hate mail can be very upsetting. I've known highly experienced broadcasters get depressed for days after having received particularly unpleasant personal attacks. If you receive a threat of physical violence you must refer this to your management and even the police. Otherwise, try not to let such mail get to you. Most of the people who write this stuff won't do anything. They are just shedding their sickness onto you. I know this is easy to say...it's a lot more difficult to cope with when confronted with the reality of a particularly nasty letter. But this is something which goes with the job and you will have to get used to it as best you can.

- Get into the habit of keeping the broadcasting desk tidy. Even in fully computerised studios you will need bits of paper. In less than modern set-ups you will, if you are not careful, find yourself drowning in cue-sheets, press releases, 'talk-up' sheets and all the rest of it as the programme goes on. Develop a system. Papers which you don't have to refer to again go in one place, cues to be used go somewhere else, and so on. If you don't do this, inevitably crises will occur when you can't find that vital piece of paper.
- Think about the way you dress. Most stations these day have some sort of dress code, but if yours doesn't consider the impression you want to make. If you dress over-formally this may well help intimidate less experienced guests. On the other hand, if you present your programme dressed in off-the-peg Oxfam your guests may find it difficult to take you seriously. You should aim at smart informality. Remember that you are the station's representative and that your appearance matters to those you interview.
- Don't let your interviewee play with pen and paper. Rustling and rattling distract listeners.
- Dissuade people from using notes or scripts. It's a rare interviewee who doesn't sound as if they're reading.
- Always remember that there are people listening to the radio waiting for you to offend them. Animal jokes and badly placed discs in relation to news stories generate the biggest response.

Tutorial

1. Name five songs that would possibly be inappropriate songs to play after the death of a celebrity.
2. Why should you never give the public your home address or phone number?
3. What should you do if you receive hate mail?

Seminar discussion

Graham Lawlor, the author and radio broadcaster said, 'I have a PO Box number and a business line as well as the household phone line. This is expensive but it is worth it for peace of mind, I have these details on my business card because the malicious are not all locked up, some of them are out there'.

Discuss this with your partner. Should you have a PO Box number? What about a separate business phone line? What about a fax line?

Resources and References

Books

Asa Briggs, *A History of Broadcasting in the United Kingdom* (Oxford University Press). This is a magisterial, multi-volume work which is great for dipping into and contains much that is interesting about the origin and development of local broadcasting.

Asa Briggs, *The BBC: The First 50 Years* (Oxford University Press). Again, interesting information about the BBC's decision to launch local radio and the re-vamp of its radio networks in 1967.

Humphrey Carpenter, *The Envy of the World: Fifty Years of the BBC Third Programme and Radio 3, 1946 1996* (Phoenix Giant). Radio 3 is not, of course, everyone's cup of tea. But this book provides a comprehensive sense of how a single radio service, admittedly an unusual one, has changed and developed down the years.

John Cole, *As It Seemed to Me* (Phoenix). The inside story of British politics from Macmillan to Major by a former Political Editor of the BBC and one of the country's most distinguished political commentators.

Robin Day, *Grand Inquisitor* (Weidenfeld and Nicolson). The memoirs of the man who invented hard interviewing.

Paul Donovan, *All Our Todays* (Jonathan Cape). A fascinating history of the BBC's *Today* programme since its launch in 1957. Apart from anything else this gives a useful sense of the development of interviewing styles.

Paul Donovan, *The Radio Companion* (Grafton). This A to Z reference guide to radio from its inception to the time of publication (1991) is invaluable. Sadly it is out of print and a new, updated edition is badly needed.

Robert Robinson, *Skip All That: Memoirs* (Century). A very entertaining book by a well known broadcaster. His chapter on his time co-presenting the Today programme is particularly informative.

Post-graduate journalism courses

Many universities offer post-graduate courses in journalism and broadcast journalism. The best are recognised by the Broadcast Journalism Training Council and offer training/support from local media. This last consideration is all important. You need to look for courses which offer practical 'on the job' placements and teaching. What follows is a selection of universities which provide popular post-graduate broadcast journalism courses. It is not a comprehensive list and you should do some research of your own.

Cardiff University, P.O. Box 494/5, Cardiff CF1 3XD. Tel: (029) 2087 4000. *www.cf.ac.uk*

University of Central England, Perry Bar, Birmingham B42 2SU.

Tel: (0121) 331 5000. *www.uce.ac.uk*

University of Central Lancashire, Preston, Lancashire PR1 2HE. Tel: (01772) 201 201. *www.uclan.ac.uk*

Goldsmiths College, University of London, New Cross, London SE14 6NW. Tel: (020) 7919 7171. *www.goldsmiths.ac.uk*

Falmouth College of Arts, Wood Lane, Falmouth, Cornwall TR11 4RH. Tel: (01326) 211 077. *www.falmouth.ac.uk*

London College of Printing, Elephant and Castle, London SW1 6SB. Tel: (020) 7514 6569. *www.lcp.linst.ac.uk*

University of Portsmouth, University House, Winston Churchill Avenue, Portsmouth PO1 2UP. Tel: (023) 9287 6543. *www.port.ac.uk*

Sheffield Hallam University, Howard Street, Sheffield S1 1WB. Tel: (0114) 225 5555. *www.shu.ac.uk*

Trinity and All Saints College, Brownberrie Lane, Horsforth. Leeds LS18 SHD. Tel: (0113) 283 7100. *www.tasc.ac.uk*

University of Westminster, 309 Regent Street, London W1R 8AL. Tel: (020) 711 500. *www.wmin.ac.uk*

Useful websites

Radio

www.radionow.co.uk The latest industry news, facts and features from around the country. You can find the stations in your area using an interactive map. The site lists every radio station in the country and provides links to their sites.

www.ukradio.com News about UK radio. You can sign up for the weekly e-mail radio newsletter, a useful digest of industry news.

www.mediauk.com Independent online media directory. Amongst other features, the site lists all local, hospital and student stations.

www.hbauk.com The website of the Hospital Broadcasting Association, containing advice on how to get involved in hospital radio and an explanation of the work of the HBA.

Current affairs

All national newspapers have their own websites which provide more information about the stories they have printed and useful links.

Daily Mail *www.dailymail.co.uk*
Daily Express *www.express.co.uk*
The Guardian *www.guardian.co.uk*
The Independent *www.independent.co.uk*
The Mirror *www.mirror.co.uk*

Daily Telegraph *www.telegraph.co.uk*
The Times *www.thetimes.co.uk*

www.informationchannel.co.uk is a UK directory of links to all the best news and current affairs websites. Very useful indeed.
www.aij_uk.com is the site of the Association of Investigative Journalists. This is a global organisation based in London promoting investigative journalism. The site publicises recent stories of scandal and corruption.

For breaking news, you can consult sites run by news gathering organisations including television companies. There are a number of these but I have found the following most useful.

BBC *www.new.bbc.co.uk*
ITN *www.itn.co.uk*
Reuters *www.reuters.com*
PA Newswire *www.pa.press.net*

Politics and government

The three main national parties have websites with information about their policies, latest initiatives and campaigns, speeches and so on.

Labour *www.labour.org.uk*
Conservative *www.conservatives.com/home.cfm.home*
Liberal Democrat *www.libdems.org.uk*

www.number-10.gov.uk The Number 10 site of course puts the best possible spin on recent government initiatives but does have useful information on the legislative process and other parliamentary matters. Much more useful is *www.open.gov.uk* which provides a single point of entry for people who want government information.

Also useful is the National Statistics site found at *www.statistics.gov.uk* This contains the latest comprehensive range of official UK statistics. Inevitably, it's rather dry but it's surprisingly easy to navigate. Amongst useful information it provides the latest economic indicators and population estimates. Material is added almost daily.

The government's ministries all have websites which explain areas of ministerial responsibility, publish policies, ministerial statements and other relevant matters.

Home Office *www.homeoffice.gov.uk*
Foreign and Commonwealth Office *www.fco.gov.uk* (The Foreign and Commonwealth Office also has a site which concentrates on human rights as a guiding principle in policy making. *www.hrpd.fco.gov.uk*)
Treasury *www.hm.treasury.gov.uk*
Department for Education and Employment *www.dfee.gov.uk*
Department of Health *www.doh.gov.uk*
Department of the Environment, Transport and the Regions *www.detr.gov.uk*
Department of Culture, Media and Sport *www.culture.gov.uk*
Lord Chancellor's Department *www.open.gov.uk/lcd/lcdhome.htm*

www.royal.gov.uk The official website of the British Monarchy. It contains a history of the monarchy, diaries of engagements etc.

The European Union has a plethora of sites but the three most useful in my experience are:

www.cec.org.uk The site of the European Commission Representation in the UK. It contains information about EU policy as it applies in the UK, EU tenders, directories of EU institutions and other matter.
www.europarl.en.int The site of the European Parliament. It contains details of membership, agendas and meetings.
www.openupeurope.com The citizen's guide to the European Parliament. It supplies much useful documentation and links to other sites.

Government agencies

DSS *www.dss.gov.uk* Contains details of all social security benefits set out in a very easy to understand fashion.
www.targetingfraud.gov.uk Outlines DSS activities in tackling fraud, the site includes a confidential online fraud allegation reporting form.
www.bfi.gov.uk Explains the work of the Independent Benefit Fraud Inspectorate. The regional reports are useful.
Inland Revenue *www.inlandrevenue.gov.uk* News and information on tax and national insurance matters in the UK.

Eight campaigning websites

As you search for information, talking points and unusual perspectives on stories you will, of course, discover dozens of useful websites. Here are just eight websites that I frequently consult either to look up specific information or to see what the latest developments are.

Age Concern *www.ace.org.uk* The main organisation campaigning for a better deal for older people.
Alternative medicine *www.pitt.edu/~cbw/altm* This is a comprehensive jumpstation for sources of information on unconventional, unorthodox, alternative and complementary therapies.
Amnesty *www.amnesty.org.uk* The highly respected organisation which protests at human rights abuses around the world.
Charter 88 *www.charter88.org.uk* The campaign for reform of democracy.
Council for the Protection of Rural England *www.cpre.org.uk* Mounts frequent campaigns to sustain the country's rural areas.
Countryside Alliance *www.countryside-alliance.org* Concentrates on the arguments for continuing hunting.
Earth Times *www.earthtimes.org* An independent, international, non-partisan newspaper on the environment. The site changes daily.
League Against Cruel Sports *www.league.uk.com* Together with the Countryside Alliance website this provides a useful sense of the state of play in the hunting debate.

Appendix: NUJ Code of Conduct

I reproduce here relevant parts of the NUJ code of conduct for journalists. This provides a useful guide to how you should conduct yourself in the course of your job.

- A journalist has a duty to maintain the highest professional and ethical standards.
- A journalist shall at all times defend the principle of the freedom of the press and other media in relation to the collection of information and expression of comment and criticism. He/she shall strive to eliminate distortion, news suppression and censorship.
- A journalist shall strive to ensure that the information he/she disseminates is fair and accurate, avoid the expression of comment and conjecture as established fact and falsification by distortion, selection or misrepresentation.
- A journalist shall rectify promptly any harmful inaccuracies, ensure that correction and apologies receive due prominence and afford the right of reply to persons criticised when the issue is of sufficient importance.
- A journalist shall obtain information only by straightforward means. The use of other means can be justified only by overriding considerations of public interest. The journalist is entitled to exercise a personal conscientious objection to the use of such means.
- A journalist shall do nothing which entails intrusion into anybody's private life, grief or distress subject to justification by overriding considerations of the public interest.
- A journalist shall protect confidential sources of information.
- A journalist shall not accept bribes nor shall he/she allow other inducements to influence the performance of his/her professional duties.
- A journalist shall not lend himself/herself to the distortion or suppression of the truth because of advertising or other considerations.
- A journalist shall mention a person's age, sex, race, colour, creed, illegitimacy, disability, marital status, or sexual orientation only if this information is strictly relevant. A journalist shall never originate nor process material which encourages discrimination, ridicule, prejudice or hatred on any of the above-mentioned grounds.
- A journalist shall not take private advantage of information gained in the course of his/her duties before the information is public knowledge.
- A journalist shall not by way of statement, voice or appearance endorse by advertisement any commercial product or service save for the promotion of his/her own work or the medium by which he/she is employed.

Index

active listening, 17ff
Age Concern, 63
Amos, Geoff, 102–3

BBC Asian Network, 25
BBC Producer Guidelines, 64, 67, 90
BBC Radio 5, 23, 24, 93
BBC Radio 4FM, 55, 102, 103
BBC Radio GMR, 104
BBC Radio Leicester, 23, 67, 102, 103, 104
BBC London Live, 25
BBC Radio 3FM, 102
BBC Radio 2FM, 26, 102, 113
BBC Radio WM, 24, 46, 79
Belgrano, 75
Briggs, Asa, 101
Byrne, Gay, 61

Campaign for the Protection of Rural England, 63
Campus radio, 20
Capital Radio, 105
Charter 88, 63
Child Poverty Action Group, 63
Clarke, Kenneth, 61
Classic FM, 16
Cole, John, 64–5
contempt, 88ff
cue writing, 32ff

Day, Sir Robin, 50ff, 55, 57, 59, 65
defamation, 82ff
Derbyshire, Victoria, 24
Deol, Sonia, 24–26
Diana, Princess of Wales, 98
Donovon, Paul, 9, 61
Doolan, Ed, 79

England, Steve, 21–2

Frost, Sir David, 61

Gilbert and Sullivan, 32
Gillard, Frank, 100ff, 107
Gould, Diana, 75–6
Gowrie, Lord, 86–7
Green, Victoria, 104

Heffer, Simon, 51
hospital radio, 20, 21ff
Howard, Michael, 57
'heritage radio', 72
Humphreys, John, 55, 60, 61, 65

impartiality, 64ff
Institute of Chartered Accountants, 110
interviewing, hard, 94ff
interviews, phone/down the line, 40–1
interviews, preparing for, 31ff

Kennedy, Sir Ludovic, 57
Kipling, Rudyard, 92

LBC, 105

McCartney, Paul, Sir 79
McGarry, Sue, 23
Midlands Today, 23
Monty Python's Life of Brian, 63
Mosey, Roger, 55, 60

National Insurance, 112
Newsnight, 55

Oak FM, 106

Panorama, 50
Paxman, Jeremy, 30, 51, 55, 57, 58, 59, 60, 65
Pebble Mill, 25
pensions, 111
Pope, Alexander, 12
Precott, John, 104
pressures of broadcasting, 93ff
phone-ins, production of, 69
presenters, qualities needed by, 10ff
pressure groups, 63–4

questions, closed, 42ff
questions, open, 42ff

Radio Luxembourg, 105
Radio XL Birmingham, 25
Robinson, Robert, 52–3

SAGA Radio, 107
Savage, Don, 62
Smith, John, 97–8
Spire FM, 106
Steve Wright in the Afternoon, 26
Sunrise Radio, 25

Thatcher, Baroness Margaret, 75–6, 79, 97, 98
Today, 52, 55, 56, 61
Transport 2000, 63
Trelinksi, Alex, 115–6

Virgin Radio, 16
vox pops, 36

Wadsworth, Tony, 46f
Walden, Brian, 53f
Wark, Kirsty, 30, 65
Weekend World, 53
Worricker, Julian, 23–4, 93